DEDICATION

This book is dedicated to all Sundancers,
no matter where they dance.
All men, women and children who have gone
to the Sacred Tree to pray.

I wrote this to honor them and in
respect to our Sundance.

*This book is in
honor of my Mother*

Helen T. Rendon

and in

*Memory of my Father
Manuel M. Rendon
(to whom I dedicated my Sundance in 1994)*

MY ROAD TO THE SUNDANCE

By

Manny Twofeathers

X

Wo-Pila Publishing
Phoenix, Arizona

Library of Congress Catalog Card Number: 94-90673

Twofeathers, Manny
    My Road to the Sundance

ISBN 1-886340-04-8

TABLE OF CONTENTS

DEDICATION
ACKNOWLEDGEMENTS
INTRODUCTION

THE SEVEN DIRECTIONS

ACKNOWLEDGEMENTS

I want to show my respect by honoring the Spirits of all the Sacred Directions. They brought me all I needed to find my way to the Sundance.

All the people I have met in this new direction in my life. I would like to thank each and every one. You know who you are, so many of you are mentioned. "Wo-Pila" - I am deeply grateful.

Also a special thank you for the lady who took the picture on the cover of this book, who promised she would send it and did. We hope she will come forward so we can give her proper credit.

Included is my family, especially Rockie, Stormy, Mary, Becky, Dory and Oriona who gave me so much confidence and support while I was writing this book. A big thank you to my mother-in-law, Lynne Babuin for her much appreciated help. Our dear friend Sharon Passero, who was always there when we needed her and has always encouraged me. Also a big thank you to Tom Fuchs for last minute editing that saved the final text!

And finally I want to honor my wife, Melody, (formerly Betty Hutton) for her excellent memory, editing this book, expertise at the computer, endless hours at it and her love, devotion and patience with me.

INTRODUCTION

What is the Sundance?

"The Sundance is our way of sacrificing
ourselves for the privilege of having a direct
connection with the creator. It is a special
ceremony brought to us to give thanks and show
gratitude. A way to humble ourselves, pray for
the healing of others and ask for a better way of
life for everyone.
A spiritual awakening for some, and a spiritual
commitment for others." M.T. '94

I had attended a few Sundances for several years,
but never as a participant. Whenever I heard of one,
I felt compelled to go and be around this energy, like
a moth to a light. I never understood this attraction.
I'd stand for hours where I could see the dancers,
and wonder why they did this? When I left, I felt
sad and empty. I couldn't understand that feeling.
The first Sundance that I ever saw was being held
in Fort Duchesne, Utah. The Ute people hold what
is called a *Thirst* Sundance. They go through four
full days of hard dancing and praying without
anything to drink or eat the entire time. It is
extremely hard just to complete the ceremony. The
constant blowing on the Eagle Whistle, dehydrates
the dancers very quickly and the four days are made
almost intolerable by the thirst.
I asked for and received permission to sell my
crafts. After the first day I realized my heart wasn't
in selling, because in the distance I could hear the
singers, the drum and the eagle whistles. They
appeared to be calling me to the Sundance Arbor.
For two days I stood watching the dancers and
praying. It was great just being there. My spirit felt

light as if wanting to fly. Then reality set in, I had to earn a living, so I left.

A few weeks later I found myself back in Ft. Duchesne, long after the Sundance was over. Driving by, there was a strong urge to go to the Sundance Arbor. With butterflies in my stomach I turned off the main highway. I didn't know why I was going there, I knew no one would be there. Maybe the spirits wanted me to go by myself and feel the Sundance energy, to experience it alone. The closer I got, the more nervous I became. I kept questioning myself, wondering what I was doing there and why.

When I reached the gate leading into the Sundance grounds, I was elated to see the tree was still standing. All the offering flags were waving happily, and it still stood proudly. I don't know why, but I had the distinct impression that it was happy to see me. That it was lonely and needed my company.

I parked my van away from it respecting its sacred space. Getting out, I walked slowly to the tree. It was good to be alone with it and to have this moment of privacy. The closer I got the stronger the tree's energy became. I started feeling the sorrow, the tears and the pain from the Sundancers that had prayed here.

I had to touch it. As I touched the tree, I looked up and saw all the prayer flags and offerings, waving gently. When I did, I was overwhelmed. All those emotions and energies from the previous Sundancers, combined with its healing energy overcame me.

I started to cry. Tears formed then spilled out of my eyes. It was as though the tree needed my emotions. I gave the tree what it wanted, willingly, without shame, as I prayed.

To this day, I don't know how long I was there, but when it was over I felt an enormous relief. I didn't realize that I had been kneeling. As I stood up, I realized that I had also been under a lot of stress from my responsibilities. That Sacred Tree had paid me back for visiting it. It had given me relief from all the pressure and anxiety. As I backed away, I was humbled by the experience.

Getting closer to the van, I saw another car, it was a tribal policeman. He asked me what I was doing there and I explained that I had just come to the tree to pray. I'm sure he could see the remains of emotions on my face. Understanding, he quietly told me it was okay. He asked if I was a Sundancer, and I said no. He said he understood my wanting to pray because he was a Sundancer. He understood the power of the tree and why I wanted to pray. We talked for a little while longer. He wished me well then I left.

Driving away, I was exhilarated with happiness. I wanted to shout out my experience and let the world know of my joy.

As a part Native and part mixed ancestry from the Southwest, this ceremony was not part of my culture and until this time unknown to me.

The most memorable part of the Sundance ceremony was the sound made by the Eagle Bone Whistle. If you're open to spirituality, this is one thing at a Sundance that leaves a permanent imprint on your heart and soul. The haunting sound of the Eagle Bone Whistle stays with you, no matter where you go or what you do.

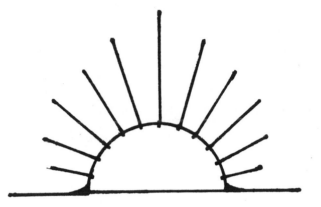

EAST - YELLOW

"New Beginnings"
Rising Sun

1985 Sacramento, California . . .

It all started about 6:30 on a Sunday morning. For two days I was displaying my silver and turquoise jewelry, at a Native American Conference that began Friday. Now it was Sunday morning.

A common native custom is to invite friends who are in town to stay at your home. I had a couple of good friends in Sacramento, Kat and Dave. They had asked me to stay with them while there.

This gave me a chance to visit and it saved me some money. I woke up early that morning, quietly took a shower, got dressed and eased myself out of the house. I figured I'd go to a restaurant close by and have a great, big breakfast. After that, get my jewelry ready and set up early.

The morning was pleasant and cool. I felt great. Today was it. I would be going home that night after the conference. I was away from home several days and started to miss my kids.

Since I got up that morning I had been feeling extraordinarily happy and couldn't understand why. I'm never cheerful that early in the morning. Especially when I haven't had my coffee.

Again I thought about how good I was feeling, "I'm going to have a fine day, that's why I feel so good." I felt a little strange and almost light headed. A couple of times I tried to analyze my feelings but it just felt too good to worry about it. Deep inside, I had a strange sensation that this was going to be a very special day somehow.

As you can well imagine, early Sunday morning there wasn't too much traffic anywhere. In that section of Sacramento, there wasn't any at all except me. I had been moving down the freeway at a pretty good clip when my exit came up fast. I slowed quickly and eased my old van off the freeway. I came to the first intersection and had to stop. The light had just turned red. I waited for the light to change back to green.

I waited and waited. I must have looked at my watch three or four times in just as many seconds. As I sat there I got a faint whiff of hot oil from the engine. I thought to myself, "I'd better watch how fast I drive this old van or I'll find myself walking."

When the oil smell disappeared, so did thoughts of the van's condition. My thoughts drifted, I wondered if that day was going to be better than the day before. Again I noticed that the engine sounded pretty good. It was idling really smooth and easy.

My mind returned to the present. Starting to get a little irritated, I thought, "When is this @#$%^&* light going to change?" I looked around, then glanced into my rear view mirror, thinking, "If there's no cops around I'm going to go on and cross."

Then I thought, "The light must be stuck or something. It's probably broken." I started dreaming up excuses I could tell the cop if I got caught running that red light. I was thinking very seriously of running it. A hundred thoughts raced through my mind as I sat there irritated at the dumb light that wouldn't change.

At times like that, I think we all act a bit childish when things don't go our way. I was starting to get to that state. I didn't want that good feeling, that I'd had all morning, changed by anything, especially a traffic light.

How long had I been waiting? It seemed an eternity. Maybe it seemed a long time because of my impatience or maybe I had been sitting there longer than normal.

By now, thoroughly disgusted, I just couldn't

understand why this was happening to me.

I was hungry. I hadn't had my first cup of coffee yet. That made my cigarettes taste terrible!

It was just not too good to keep me from my coffee . . . LIGHT! Lights or whatever just shouldn't keep a guy from the little things in life that mean so much! I'm sure you've heard about the old bear coming out of hibernation? Well that's exactly how I was starting to feel.

So why didn't the light change and let me go about my business? Impatiently, I looked at my watch again. I scanned up and down the streets, and they were empty as far as I could see. Again I'm thinking of going through the red light.

Then I think, "Ha! Ha! I'll bet there's a cop somewhere pushing the buttons that make the lights change. Just waiting for me to screw up so he can bust me. No sir, you're not going to get me that easy. I'll wait you out."

About this time, through my irritation and aggravated state I started hearing something. At first very, very softly almost like a whisper at the back of my mind or like a thought.

I started hearing a sound. Though I didn't know what it was, I thought I recognized it. I started getting chills. I don't know how to describe it. It's very hard to write a sound but I'll try. It started softly, a shrill whisper - "Sherii - Sherii - Sherii - Sherii" as it went on, it got louder and louder.

"What's that?" I thought, "Where have I heard that sound before? It sure sounds familiar. Where, where have I heard it before?" I repeatedly asked myself. It almost became painful trying to recall. It was such a beautiful and haunting sound.

Since I had an older van, I thought, "Maybe this old van is developing a new crippling symptom. God, I hope not. This old van is already worth $30,000 dollars just from repairs."

The "Sherii - Sherii - Sherii - Sherii," - sound kept getting louder and kept going on and on.

I cocked my head, turning it slowly, trying to find where the sound was coming from. It wasn't the engine. "Ha! Ha!" I thought it's the radio. I reached over and tried to turn it off. It was already off. What in the world is it? I knew I had heard that sound before. Maybe something in the back is making that sound because of vibrations from the engine.

I turned completely around in the seat. Carefully I looked at everything back there. There was nothing that could be making that sound. As I straightened out and sat back in the seat, the light was still red. Keeping me right there where I had to listen to that beautiful, eerie, haunting sound.

Suddenly, I felt goose bumps all over my body. I was having trouble swallowing. I felt as if something had gripped me by the throat. My heart was having trouble deciding whether to stop beating or to jump out of my chest. I didn't know what was going on, but I knew deep inside my soul that a very special message was coming to me.

I had finally recognized the sound. I felt myself covered by a warm, quiet mixture of sound and peaceful energy. A great sigh escaped from my long held breath. I knew without any doubt what I was hearing. It was not one, but several Eagle wing bone whistles. Exactly like at the Sundances where I had always heard them!

"But, I'm not at a Sundance! This is 6:30 A.M. on a Sunday morning in Sacramento," I thought. Full realization was hitting me. I broke into a sweat, thinking why me? What does it mean?

Suddenly I was no longer in my van in Sacramento. In my mind I was swiftly transported to that Sacred Sundance Tree so far away. To that lonely tree in Ft. Duchesne where I had prayed and felt so much emotion. Again I was kneeling at its base in prayer with my hands on its rough bark. I could hear it talking to me.

I distinctly heard the words meant for me, "you have searched long enough. It is time that you look to us for your destiny and direction. There is much to do." I didn't think about where I was or what I was doing. My thoughts were of how soft the voice was and I wondered what it meant. I couldn't quite understand what was happening to me.

Suddenly I was back in my van at the traffic light. I looked around confused.

Had I been day dreaming?

Had I really been to the tree?

Had all this happened to me for a reason?

As I set there confused and a little scared. I looked down at my hands and although I couldn't see anything, I swear I could still feel the tree's rough bark. Had I really been there or had my thoughts been so real I could feel reality with my mind?

You might think, "So what's the big deal about thinking that you've heard Eagle whistles or had a vision? Why would it make you go through all the different body emotions?" It's one of those things that's hard to explain, yet very real to native people. Though many of us get away from our ancient beliefs, I suppose we never really lose it. It's deeply ingrained in our genes. Possibly, it's part of our D.N.A. if that's at all possible.

It takes an occurrence like this to return a native person to their old beliefs. The fear didn't come from dread of what could happen because of what I had heard. It was just a fear of the unknown.

I believe that all of us have experienced those little shivers of unexplainable feelings. That's what was happening to me that morning. That sound and thoughts of the Sundance were now freshly burned into my brain again. The soft voice that had spoken to me, had left me badly shaken. It felt as though I had been at the Sundance Tree in person.

Coming out of it as if from a dream, I shook my head. Unknown to me, a car had pulled up behind me and softly honked its horn. I looked up. The light had changed to green. Putting the van in gear, I slowly crossed the street and continued to the restaurant.

As I entered it, I was still, I guess, in a sort of daze. The waitress asked, "Are you okay, sir?"

"Sure," I answered, "I'm fine." I didn't understand what had happened in that few moments or was it hours, at the light? I did know that something very important had happened to me. Somehow I knew that it was going to change my life in a big way.

Since then, I have come to realize, this was my first vision! It was as if the Spirits were telling me it was time to return to my native spirituality. They were showing me the way. After understanding what I was seeing, I had the freedom to choose if I wanted to follow it or not.

I feel this came to me because it was something I needed. I spent the day as if in a daze. I couldn't stop thinking about the morning. I'm not sure but I bet that I gave some pretty good bargains that day! Financially it had been a very good day, indeed.

After the show ended that Sunday evening, I drove back home. I took Highway 99 straight south and got off on Highway 120. Driving through Oakdale was a breeze. I think I hit one red light and was through before I knew it. I headed east into the foothills of the sierras. It was late when I reached the town of Sonora.

It had been sprinkling a little in the foothills earlier. The road was still wet. The tires sounded like they were singing as I drove along. As I left Sonora behind me I realized that I was almost home. Where did time go? My mind wandered, thinking about my vision, I hardly felt the trip. My mind was still full of the Eagle whistles.

Arriving home, I found my wife waiting up for me. She had hot coffee ready. As she poured me a cup, she asked my how the weekend had gone. It didn't take long to tell her that I'd had a good weekend, but I wanted to tell her about my experience. I tried to explain what had happened. I suppose she understood, but I could see that she didn't understand the importance of the occurrence. She took it very lightly.

I tried to tell her how I had felt receiving this spiritual visit. I tried to explain the confusion, fear, apprehension, and joy that I felt. I couldn't make myself understood.

Anyways, after that, I became very inquisitive and aggressive trying to find out about the Sundance. I knew absolutely nothing about it. I guess that in my anxiety to find out, I approached some people the wrong way. I found myself not being able to get answers from anyone.

I'm going to retrace my life a few years to let you know about how I was spiritually.

I had none! I felt lost!

I was born and reared a Catholic, through no choice of mine. I thought that was pretty neat when a bunch of us kids had classes on things like how to behave in church and other lessons. Going into the church was always a little scary to me, I could never talk aloud. We felt that we had to talk in a whisper. The teachers who taught us made us feel important. It was probably a form of brainwashing. They were getting us ready to do the church's bidding as we grew older. They were teachers during the week, and on weekends they would be partying and drinking.

My parents had a restaurant for many years. The "after the bar closed" crowd would always go there to eat. I saw many of the same people, my teachers and pillars of the community, drunk, fighting, staggering and falling.

When I was ten years old, I decided to become an altar boy. They use either one or two boys to help the priest when he holds Mass services. I did this for several months. I would get up early in the morning, ride my bike to town about three miles away. I would sell newspapers to men going to work. I'd make two cents off each paper I sold for ten cents!

With that little job done, I would go to the church and get my black and white altar boy gown on. Then I'd light candles and do all my other little tasks to get ready for the 7:30 am Mass.

It always seemed so majestic in the church. It was always so quiet, peaceful, and scary in there. I never liked the smell of candles. It reminded me of funerals. I was always curious to see what the priest was doing behind the great big altar. That was where we got ready, before mass.

I watched as the priest performed his daily ritual. At the time it seemed like quite a ceremony to get his habit on. I would stand wide eyed, not wanting to move a muscle while he did his thing. Now that I'm older and think about it, I think he went to the bottle more than the ceremony called for. But, then what do I know?

After mass, I would head for school. The altar boys would meet once a week, Saturdays I think. So as it happened on the meeting day of that week, we got a new, young priest. I was sick and couldn't make it to the meeting. I stayed sick over the weekend and didn't even go to church Sunday.

When the following meeting came around, I was there, but the new priest wasn't. I still hadn't met him. Sunday morning after selling my papers, I went dutifully to church. There were several of us altar boys. So, we took turns helping the priests.

That Sunday was not my turn. When I got there,

I found the priest standing in front of the church. He appeared worried while looking up and down the street. He was controlling his irritation.

When I walked up, I said good morning. He answered kind of gruffly. I asked what was wrong, he replied that the altar boys had not shown up. He said he needed to start Mass immediately. Though he had never met or seen me before. I offered to help him. He turned angrily at me and between clenched teeth he said, "What the hell do you know about being an altar boy?"

He didn't even wait to hear my answer, just turned and walked back into the church. I stood there dumbfounded. All I could think was, this is the man who was above reproach? This is the man I'm supposed to respect and follow? Everything I had learned since childhood evaporated in a matter of seconds that morning in front of the church.

I stood there for a moment, torn between the truth just revealed to me and fear of the punishment I was going to get if I didn't go to church. The truth won out. This single event made me wonder, even with my young mind, how much was truth and how much was not! I said a prayer to the Gods or whomever was in charge, not to hold it against me. I walked away from the Catholic Church and have never returned.

Well, there was just one instance that I did go back into the same church. We lost my dad recently. The services were at that church. The service disgusted me. It started well enough, I suppose, with the priest bringing out my father's good points, the usual litany about how much he would be missed. Then he turned my father's service into a recruiting exercise. He told us that it was too bad that we had to come back to church under these circumstances.

He went on to say that at least we were back in the church, and that we should continue to come to

Mass. He carried on and on in the same recruiting mode for several minutes.

I guess in his own twisted way of thinking, it made sense. It made me angry to see that none of the others saw it the way I did, except my wife. She was angry, too!

Later, I had looked into the Baptist Christian faith. I was only there to meet girls. It was fun for a few months, however I realized that was not what I was looking for, so I stopped going. Don't misunderstand me, girls are beautiful and I love them, but I was thirsty for spirituality.

Somewhere along this time in my life I left all this. Disappointed in Christianity, I became a guy looking for thrills and good times. I became buddies with a couple of friends and we ended up in Seattle, Washington.

Once after work, I was walking back to my apartment, when these two people stopped to talk to me. They were both Japanese people, one was an older man and the other a middle age woman. They smiled very politely, bowed and greeted me.

I was a little apprehensive because in big cities when people smile at you they usually want something. So, with a bit of reservation I said hello. They asked me, if I had ever been to a Buddhist meeting, while handing me a pamphlet. I said, "No, I don't even know what you mean."

It was a little hard to understand what they were trying to tell me, but I was ripe for the picking. Disenchanted by Christianity, I was open to anything else that might come along!

For instance, once while I was partying, I tried toking and doing light smoke. I never got into that. I would choke really bad with it, then when it took hold of me, I just wanted to go to sleep or get sick. That didn't hold my interest very long.

The Japanese couple found me, interested so they

really poured it on. They convinced me that I should attend their meetings. So, I did! I found it very interesting and different. I tried to be serious and faithful to this new belief.

After several weeks, I got bored with it. I believe it might have been because I didn't understand enough of it. It was just too different. I still respect it, but I was just starting to use it in a selfish way. I decided not to use any faith in that manner. I stopped going to the meetings. I should explain what I mean about using it selfishly.

One main thing they identified with in this faith, was whatever you wanted, all you had to do, is focus on it, while you chanted a very old chant, *"Nam-yo-ho-ran-ge-kyo."* The sound emitted when you said it made a vibration. A vibration that enabled you to connect with the universe and receive anything you desired. So, of course, I was always chanting for girls, booze and parties.

Boy, did it work! For a long time after leaving Seattle, I was burned out on booze and parties, but I never got tired of girls.

Another thing happened in my past. Once I was a CB nut and had one of those radios, truckers use to talk with each other mounted in my van. Everybody who uses them has a "handle." At the time, I knew nothing about the Sundance. For some unknown reason I adopted the name "Sundancer" as my C.B. handle! Was it premonition or were the spirits making me aware of the word as if preparing me for it?

Shortly after the occurrence in Sacramento, I had a burning desire to learn more about the Sundance. Oddly enough, though I had been to several of them, I suddenly realized that I hadn't made any close friendships with anyone at any of the Sundances.

When the Eagle whistles sounded for me in Sacramento, we had been living on the Tuoloumne

Mi-wok Rancheria. It's a small reservation not far from Sonora, California. Shortly after that our lease on our rental house ran out and we decided to move.

The place we ended up was Blackfoot, Idaho. I really don't know why we moved there, except that there are many native people there who bead. Some of the best beadwork in the country comes from that area. We were the only people in this country that knew how to cut (facet) beads. So we had a good market.

Our life in Blackfoot, Idaho wasn't much different from anywhere else. We made crafts, cut beads and I went on the road to sell them.

Another big event happened in June. My little Dorina was born in Pocatello, Idaho. Her birth was at the beginning of my Sundance journey.

Once I went to a Sundance at Fort Washakie, Wyoming, where they were allowing craft people to set up. We could sell in an area that was quite a distance from the Sundance Arbor. After deciding to go to Fort Washakie I suddenly started feeling a funny little sensation in the pit of my stomach. I didn't know what was wrong with me but almost lost my desire to go there. I felt a little bit afraid and apprehensive. It was as though I knew that by going there my spiritual quest would become clear, a new path. Maybe I feared what I might find.

I left Blackfoot early in the morning and stopped in Idaho Falls to buy groceries for my few days in Ft. Washakie. Later I ate lunch in Jackson Hole, Wyoming, then passed by the Grand Tetons and the southern tip of Yellowstone Park. Between there and Dubois, Wyoming, must be some of the most beautiful scenery in the world. It seems as though the Creator was either in a very good mood when he made that area or he had time on his hands and was feeling creative. He did a great job.

The afternoon that I drove in to the Arapaho

Sundance, the weather was hot and sticky. When I stopped the van, it felt as if the heat comprised of tiny little hot hammers, trying to beat me down.

I got out of the van. I stretched and felt the full force of the sun. Then I thought of the guys that were going in to Sundance, and how hot it was going to be. I felt sorry for them. Little did I know, that soon I would be one of them.

I went over to check on the set up. The guy in charge was not too friendly and they wanted too much for a space. So I decided to get a tribal permit for $20.00 that was good for a year. Then I could set up anywhere on the reservation. Much, much better!

I set up at an intersection away from the Sundance. That's where I met Allen. He was to be the one who introduced me to the Sundance, my "Grandfather." We use the word "Grandfather" for different reasons. It is a word to refer to "God" or to someone we respect very much. Or a person who sponsors, or introduces another person into the Sundance.

I had lots of my cut beads laid out. There has always been just two places to get cut beads, in Czechoslovakia or Japan. So when we started cutting beads some people just couldn't believe that we knew how to cut them. We took pride in cutting them. So when Allen walked up, he was surprised at how many I had.

He remarked, "Boy, the Japs are sure cutting a lot of beads, and all sizes too."

Japanese cuts are considered inferior to the Czech cuts. His tone of voice was almost on the verge of being sarcastic.

Instantly, I became defensive, my hackles ruffled. "I beg your pardon," I said indignantly, "We cut these beads."

Allen looked a little surprised by my aggressive reply.

Thank God, he had the presence of mind to calm himself. I noticed that he did start to make another comment, but stopped. I found out later that he's a pretty tough character. Not because he told me, but because I know a warrior when I see one.

He said, "Sorry, didn't mean to offend you!"

That, set me back a little, I apologized for the outburst. I explained how I'd heard that in the past and it upset me quite a bit if someone compared ours to Japanese cuts.

Once things smoothed out, I found out Allen was not a bad sort. I'm glad that one of us had some common sense. This time around, it had not been me.

We visited awhile, talking about mutual interests. I told him about my family, he told me about his, then he left.

The following day in the afternoon, Allen came back to see me. I asked him if he knew where I could get some Eagle feathers. He replied that, he had brought me some. From his car he brought me a large paper sack and gave it to me. It felt good receiving those feathers. I asked him what I could give him in return, or what did I owe him?

"Nothing at all, I don't sell Eagle feathers," he replied.

Understand that during this period of my life, I knew nothing about traditions. I didn't realize the importance and significance of Eagle feathers to our people. Here I was completely ignorant, offering to pay for something sacred. Now it was my turn to apologize to him.

"It's okay," he said, "you didn't know, and it's a gift from me to you."

"So I can give you a gift if I want to?" I asked. Now I was being more careful on how I said things.

"I didn't do that so I could get something in return," he answered back.

"Well I want you to take these to your wife," I said. I gave her cut beads of each color that I had. I had quite a few different colors and sizes. That exchange of gifts helped to start a friendship that has lasted for years.

Before Allen left, I asked him why he decided to give me those feathers. He replied that he didn't know. He just had a feeling that I was going to need them pretty soon.

Then I remembered my quest, or desire to know about the Sundance. So I asked, "Allen do you know any Sundancers or anyone connected to the Sundance?"

"Why do you ask?"

"I was told that I had to Sundance," I replied.

"By whom?   Who told you, you had to Sundance?"

"Man, I really don't know."   Then I proceeded to tell him of what had happened to me in California.

"You're right, it sounds like you were being told to do a Sundance," he replied after much thought. "So what are you going to do about it?"

"Well, I want to go into a Sundance, but everyone I ask, won't talk to me about it."

"How serious are you about dancing?" Allen asked me.

"Well, I don't know, the Spirits said I had to do it. I guess if I can find someone to help me or teach me, I'd do it."

He said, "I'm a Sundancer and if you're serious about this, be here by the last Sunday in July."

"What do I have to bring?"

"Nothing, just bring yourself. I'll call you the week before to see if you've changed your mind or if you still want to go."

It was getting late and I started packing my things up. Allen helped me. We said our goodbyes and I left Fort Washakie.

I was very excited because I had finally found someone to help me. This whole meeting reminded me of the old proverb, "*When the student is ready, the teacher will appear.*" I was looking for someone to teach me about the Sundance, but he didn't appear until I was ready. Now I had found a Sundance and a Sundancer. I wondered why Allen said he'd call a week before to see if I still wanted to go.

I returned to Blackfoot and continued working. There wasn't a day that went by that I didn't think about the Ceremony. Most times when I was driving to and from Pow-wows or a show, I would get so scared that I would start praying. Understand that I still didn't know what I was getting into. Scared? Yes, you bet. Now that I had made this very important commitment. Do you know what scared me? Fear of failing! I was too ignorant to be scared of anything else.

I'm glad I didn't know about the thirst.

I'm glad I didn't know of the hunger and the long, hot hours spent under the blazing sun. I'm also glad I didn't know that when you dance once, you commit yourself for four years! If I had known all these things, I wondered to myself, if I would I have had the courage. Would I have had the will power, and the strength to go through it all?

Yes! I wanted to Sundance no matter what.

Good to his word, a week before the Sundance, Allen called. I told him we were leaving that day to come to Fort Washakie.

We pulled in later that night and stayed at "Rocky Acres" campground, between Fort Washakie and Landers, Wyoming. The next day Allen came after us and led us to the Sundance grounds. It took two days to set up camp. We had to go long distances to cut a certain type of bush, used for walls and shade around the camp.

This is a tradition for both the Shoshoni and the

Arapaho. They are the two tribes that live on the Fort Washakie Reservation.

After making camp, we started gathering wood for the Sweat Lodge. We had four days of purification and prayer. We would have a four-round sweat at least once a day. They were good hot sweats.

I should take this opportunity to clarify what I mean by Sweat Lodge and purification. The purification ceremony takes place in the "Sweat Lodge." Granted, people go into it to sweat, but the main purpose is to purify. Different tribes do the Purification in different ways.

The Shoshoni people do the Sweat Lodge differently from others that I know of. The lodge was right next to a cold, clear, fast running river. It came in pretty handy because in the Shoshoni Purification Ceremony, the people can come out of the lodge between rounds and go into the river. Or they could just stand around, smoke and visit. That was just fine with me, because that was my first Purification Lodge ever!

Man was it ever a hot one! The first three days of purification are spent praying. Going into the lodge and concentrating on why we were Sundancing. We were getting ourselves mentally and physically ready. It is a hard ceremony.

Many men can be driven to the brink of insanity. Some aren't able to tolerate the thirst and hunger. That is part of the sacrifice for getting your prayers answered. Some get so thirsty and hungry that their commitments cease to mean anything to them. They will go to any lengths to satisfy their desires, if allowed. People ask me, "why do you Sundance?"

I always say, "So my prayers can be answered!" To some people it may seem quite an elaborate ceremony for just praying. Anyone can get down on their knees and say a little prayer. It takes a special person to willingly put themselves through this sacrifice. Putting your ego and personal comfort aside for a few days. However, it is a lot more than that. People have different reasons to Sundance. It means something different to everyone.

Most of us pray only when we need it and only when we're in trouble. I'm as guilty as anyone else. That is what the Sundance is really about. In the Sundance you learn the meaning of being selfless. It humbles you. Because the first obligation or rule if you will, is that you never pray for yourself. You let others pray for you.

We're not just praying for now or for today, but for the whole year and the whole world. We are praying for all humanity. We also pray for others in our family, for a sick relative or loved one. We are pleading for our brothers in the rain forests, who are losing their land, as we once lost ours. We also pray for the starving people of the world, and for abused men, women and children.

This is our way to humble ourselves to the Creator. We beg that he intervene in our behalf and help us strengthen our lives so we may live better. We're also giving thanks for all the good things that Grandfather (God) has given us up to this point in our lives.

We are all willing to sacrifice ourselves so all goes well on our mother earth. Wasn't Jesus Christ also a Sundancer? He was willing to sacrifice himself so the world would evolve into a better place through Spirituality and showing us the way. Not that I would compare myself to Jesus Christ, but his sacrifice for others did help to change the world. In his time, before he died he was a man with a prayer and a message - just like we are. Perhaps our sacrifice can help make a difference too.

Purification in the Sweat Lodge is a total body, mind and spiritual cleansing in preparation to performing any of our sacred ceremonies, especially the Sundance. Once the ceremony starts the people going through it must remain celibate. They can't even touch anyone that hasn't gone through the Sweat Lodge ceremony. Most lodges last about a half hour per round. At the beginning of each round more red hot rocks get put into the lodge, keeping it good, hot and interesting.

We spent four days relaxing, getting our Eagle whistles ready. That's when I started needing the feathers that Allen had given me weeks before. As we were sitting there working on our traditional regalia, Allen smiled and looked up at me. "See Manny, I told you that you were going to need those feathers soon."

"Yeah," I was a bit puzzled or mystified by these things happening even before I knew I was going to need them.

In the bag I found some good, long, fluffy plume feathers, perfect for my Eagle whistle. I used what I needed. As other guys came by, who were going in, I gave the others away, as needed.

I saw everybody drinking large quantities of water. Some were drinking Gatorade. I finally got curious enough to ask why everyone was drinking so much. They all turned and looked at me as if finally realizing that not everyone there knew all the rules. One other guy, Jesse, said, "You'd better drink all you can, it'll be a long time before we drink again."

There was very little conversation all that afternoon. I could feel an uneasy or nervous energy radiating off everyone. This was a serious event and they all knew how hard it was going to be. The days had been real hot. In the afternoon the ground was hot enough to burn our feet. I was the only one there, I thought, who was completely ignorant. I found out later there was quite a few going in for the first time, I was the oldest. I was in my forties, and pushing my years pretty hard.

Another thing that we did that afternoon was to eat a venison stew (deer meat). Allen's wife, Zedora, fixed a large pot of it and it was delicious. It had lots of vegetables in it, but not one grain of salt. They said that if we ate salt, it would cause us to dry out faster . . . so no salt.

Well, the day had finally arrived. This was the day that would change the rest of my life. This was the day I had been excitedly expecting, yet dreading.

The sun had finally dropped below the horizon. A frenzy of quiet activity started. Everyone was quiet and busy making their last minute touches on themselves and their Sundance outfits. The smell of the dust in the air was suddenly very prominent. Dust stirred up by bare and moccasinned feet became part of the energy and part of the special moment.

The smell of the burning wood also invaded my nostrils and became part of my memories. The smell of the bubbling venison stew mingled with the different smells of wood smoke, dust and sage. People all over were smudging themselves. The smell of humans was everywhere. Perspiration, nervousness, apprehension and even joy, have a distinct smell. They were all there. They were all creating a beautiful memory for my first Sundance.

Everybody was within themselves praying to Grandfather in their own way. The energy was charged up. There was electricity in the air surrounding us, the excitement was contagious. Everyone could feel it, the enormous energy. As I sit here writing this, the memories and the recollection of it, cause me to feel that excitement all over. What a wonderful feeling, I love it!

It was now completely dark.

Allen came up to me and said, "Well, Manny, here we are. How do you feel?"

Shaking my head I replied, "Man I can't explain

it, but I feel like I'm floating!"

"That, my friend, is the Sundance energy," he smiled.

Suddenly from off in the distance, where the Arbor was, we heard the drum. A beautiful sound mellowed by distance. Then we hear one helper yelling, "Sundancers, let's go! Come on, its time to line up!"

We walked from our camp to the Arbor. A bunch of unidentified figures wrapped in colorful Pendleton blankets. As we walked, some of us were barefooted and some were wearing their moccasins.

I need to explain something at this point. The Sundance grounds were new. For years the Sundance was right in the middle of Fort Washakie. Then, the government started building houses pretty close. As the Sundance Chief once said, "One important thing about the Sundance is that every morning we must greet the Sun as it rises. With all the houses, we can't see the sun as it comes up."

That was the main reason for changing the location for the Sundance. Besides that problem in the center of Fort Washakie, there were also drunks who came around to taunt and yell at the Sundancers. They called themselves, "good Christians."

I personally felt good about the change because I was new and it was my first Sundance. This was a new place, and it was the first Sundance at this location.

I was walking toward the Arbor, very gingerly. Not only were there many small, sharp rocks, there was cactus, they're tough on bare feet.

After assembling behind the Arbor on the west side, everybody stood in one of two lines. Of course, I was sticking as close as I could to Allen.

I found out later that Allen always picked the spot in line that would place him in the Arbor on the North side. It's the hottest and hardest place to be in the Arbor for most of the day. Lots of Sundancers avoid that spot because whoever ends up there suffers the most. Yep you guessed it, Allen and I right next to him were there for three full days.

It sure makes you appreciate a lukewarm drink of water. It doesn't have to be ice cold. It really makes you appreciate a small spot of shade or a little breeze on a hot summer day. When you get down to basics, it's surprising at how little it really takes to make you happy. If not happy, at least satisfied.

So we all lined up. Shortly after that we started walking, each line going around the Arbor. One line is led by the Sundance chief, the other by one of his helpers. Each goes around on opposites sides of the Arbor. As we rounded the Arbor, we met the other line moving in the opposite direction. We were blowing our Eagle whistles as we walked around and around. It was so dark there was no way of recognizing anyone.

It was an eerie feeling to be involved in something so strange to me. I felt that I had regressed one hundred years in time. I could see many people standing quietly, watching us prepare ourselves to enter the Arbor.

The smell of dust and sage was strong, yet comforting. It felt like a friend, something familiar. We continued our walk until we had circled four times. Then the Sundance Chief led us into the Arbor. We did not leave the Arbor from Friday night just after dark until Monday afternoon. Talking about it now, it doesn't seem like a very long time. When you're in there, every hour seems like an eternity.

I did find an escape from the suffering, though. It didn't happen for a couple of days. When I finally, did discover it, it was as if the tree, the sacred tree, had talked to me. It taught me to pray, pray and pray hard. My prayers could be answered and I could endure what I was going through. My prayers were my escape.

You know something? I had found what I was looking for. I felt such joy and peace with everything and everyone, that I didn't have time to think of my suffering. I found out that things only bother you when you pay attention to them. So, if you ignore the suffering and focus on the beauty that you wish, it changes everything.

For those three days, I went through things, what can I call them, these things that I experienced? Can I call them better changes? Can I call them sufferings or spiritual awakenings? I really don't know what to call what I experienced.

I do know one thing to be a fact, the Sundance changed my life like nothing else could have. I know, without any doubt, I'm a much better man. At least, I feel that I am and so does my family.

I won't get into the details about the Sundance, because this is not a "how to" book. I was honored when they allowed me to participate in their most sacred ceremony with them. I can only return the respect and honor, by not writing what occurs during this ceremony. If it is ever to be told, I'll let that be told by a Shoshoni elder.

So we danced and danced.

We prayed and prayed.

The first day I thought was not very difficult. Remember that everyone is different. I could see other dancers were already suffering. As time went on, it was more noticeable. We danced late that first night.

The following morning we were up early. We greeted the sun, then had a little time to prepare ourselves for the day. Sometime in midmorning we started dancing again. The sun got hot early. As the day progressed it got hotter and hotter, as we danced to and from the Sacred tree.

Before we could dance back to our place, our

feet would be burning. The sore feet from the heat or hot ground are one thing. Compounding that with bruises from the little sharp rocks and cactus stickers impaling your feet, the suffering is intensified. Add to that, the number of times we danced back and forth.

Now I knew why Allen had asked me how serious I was about dancing. He later told me that many guys say they want to Sundance. When it gets right down to it, they find all kinds of excuses why they just can't make it this time. It's very, very hard. The person who goes through the Sundance ceremony must have a very important reason.

Personally I respect all Sundancers. Sundancers are a very special breed of person. Every one of them has gone to suffer and pray willingly. I believe that no matter where the Sundance is or who is running it, they're all done for the right thing. They are all special. There is no easy Sundance. You go there to pray, suffer and you should. You should sacrifice yourself so your prayers are heard and answered.

Like one Sundance Chief used to say, "If you want to go on a picnic, take your whole family and go to the river. This is your Sundance. It's only for three days. Make the most of it. Pray and dance hard." The reason he said that was that late in the afternoon when it was the hottest, some Sundancers would sit out a few songs. There is no written rule that says a Sundancer has to dance every song. It is an individual thing.

By Sunday afternoon, everyone was getting very dry. I would try to spit and my saliva was so dry it was like rubber strings. Some of us were having trouble talking. It was so hot. The constant blowing on our Eagle whistles really dried us out even faster. Swallowing was completely out of the question, by that time there is nothing to swallow.

We always looked for a dancer who would start getting ready to collapse from heat exhaustion, hunger and dehydration. We believe that is when a Sundancer is truly close to the Creator and is very powerful spiritually. He is pulling "The Sun Power" down on himself and the whole Sundance. It is the ultimate in power and energy a person can receive during a Sundance, even if it's just for a few seconds.

This is what every Sundancer is striving for.

This is when a person receives his vision.

This is when we receive direction from the Creator.

The more people this happens to in the Sundance, the more power we all receive to get our wishes and prayers fulfilled. It is a great honor to have this happen to an individual. When a dancer is showing signs of exhaustion, he receives encouragement to keep on dancing.

The drummers pick up the beat and keep on singing and drumming. When that special dancer dances back to his spot, the other dancers push him back out.

It is a wonderful feeling and a pitiful sight to see. The person who it's happening to receives respect from everyone. If the dancer falls, many dancers that are close, rush out to touch and share his energy and power. To show our respect for what he has just been through, we pick him up gently and carry him back to his spot. If he has a little shade, we lay him down so he can rest.

The Sundance goes on.

Sometimes we have two or three different groups that drum and sing for us. So we go on and on and on. The sun beats down on us for hours.

It's so very hot.

At long last, finally the Sunday sun is reaching the end of its long hot journey across the Wyoming sky. It has finally decided to give us some rest from its fiery bright energy. Though dry, hungry and tired, we feel our spirits rise with joy. We feel the ever present evening breezes and the coolness provided by the evening shadows.

Late in the night, dancers stop and tiredly lay down on their sleeping rolls. The drummers are also showing signs of fatigue. The songs are getting slower and further apart. Finally, when there are only a few dancers left, the singers finish their last song. They get up, stretch, and by ones and twos leave the Arbor.

The sun has decided to go to bed.

The dance is over for the day. Here and there I see dancers wrap up in a sheet and head for the out-house. As I laid down thinking and praying for my children, my parents and everyone else, I looked at the beautiful stars lighting up the sky.

I think, "thank you God for all the blessings you've given me throughout my life. For my beautiful children, my brother and sisters and my wonderful parents, who have always been there for me. Most of all thank you for bringing me to this Sundance. I finally have a way to thank you for all you have given me." As I lay there giving thanks, at some point, I drifted off to sleep.

Morning arrived quietly. I heard someone cough and I came awake. Where I lay I could see through the leaves of the Arbor wall. Although they are different constellations, the stars were still shining brightly. They have a cool, regal and almost aloof look to them. They looked different to me. I'm not used to seeing this group of stars. I'm not used to waking up at this time of the morning.

Now I felt an urgency to get up. Mother nature was calling. I had to answer the call of nature the first two days of the Sundance, but I figured that was normal. This was the third day! As I left my warm blankets and felt the cool air hit me, I had to move.

I got up quick and went to the outhouse. It amazed me at how much liquid I still had to get rid of. I mean it had been three days since I had anything to drink! Well, like this one dancer said, "Just because you quit drinking, doesn't mean that your kidneys stop working!"

When I returned, everyone was in high spirits. Everyone was putting on their finest regalia. I also pulled out my best shawl, it was bright red and had an Eagle sewn on the front. I was very proud of it as Allen and his wife, Zedora, gave it to me. We wrapped them around ourselves like skirts.

The rumor started going around that we weren't going to get out until late that night. You can't believe how tough that is to hear after three days without food or water. Allen pulled me to the side and told me that the rumor always started for the discomfort of the first time Sundancers. They do go late sometimes, but this doesn't happen too often.

We had to watch the flag pole in front of the Sundance Chief's camp that was away from the Arbor. If it was all the way to the top of the pole, we would be staying late. If it was at half-mast we would get out around 12:00-1:00 in the afternoon. So therefore, some time was spent looking at the flag pole.

This was the last day.

As we danced and blew on our Eagle whistles, I could hear dancers gagging because of lack of moisture in their mouths. I was feeling pretty bad myself. Once I started retching, and couldn't stop. When I finally did, I was pretty weak and shaken, but continued dancing.

Many spectators came into the Arbor for blessings. Some dancers brought in their families and others to be blessed. It was a little beyond my understanding, but Christian ministers were coming

into the Sundance Arbor and asking the Sundance
Chief to give them blessings. In turn, they asked if
they could bless other people from their congregation
in the Sundance Arbor. It was beautiful to see the
mixing of beliefs the way it happened there. At least
I'm glad that these people have the intelligence to
recognize the Arbor as a sacred place, as sacred as
any Church, anywhere.

The morning went slowly. It seemed to stretch
until the next weekend. The sun decided to take it
easy on us poor Sundancers. Maybe it thought we
had suffered enough. The morning couldn't have
been better. It was the most pleasant of the whole
time. It eased our suffering a little.

Suddenly, Allen grabbed my arm. When I looked
at him, he pointed with his chin. It directed me to
look at the flag pole. It was flying half-mast.

"Thank you, Grandfather," I said to myself.

Suddenly the people were no longer coming into
the Arbor. The blessings were over. The energy
within the circle felt charged and exciting. Even the
spectators could feel it. People were starting to smile
and laugh. Some were holding their fists up to the
dancers. A sign of victory, as if saying, "good man,
we are proud of you."

Then the Sundance Chief tied up his sheet.

Everybody started following his example. The
sheets we had used to cover ourselves at times during
the Sundance now concealed us from the spectator's
eyes. At first I didn't understand why. Then it was
explained to me. We were about to have our first
drink of water in three days. This is sacred water to
be received with humbleness and respect. It was too
personal to be seen by anyone else, other than your
Sundance brothers and God.

They brought two large, old metal, milk cans of
fresh spring water. After bringing the water in, the
helpers placed it before the Sundance Chief. He

prayed over the water, gave thanks for it, then with his blessing he poured it into buckets. His helpers brought it to us.

One by one, they let each dancer drink his fill. It was a quiet time, filled with reverence. It felt like his own personal ceremony was taking place, as each Sundancer took his first drink. I won't say what else goes on behind the sheets because everybody reacts differently during this very important moment of their lives. I will tell you about me.

As the helpers stopped in front of me, one of them took a large dipper full of cool sweet well water out of the bucket. He raised it high enough to clear the edge of the bucket. Water splashed and dripped off the sides of it. It looked fantastically delicious. The helper was not moving fast enough. The whole process seemed to take the longest time. Every move was in slow motion.

I'm sitting on the ground watching as all this is happening. My throat felt stretched tight, as my head tilted back. I tried to swallow as I looked at that beautiful water, however, all I could do right then, is croak. The feeling was so intense that I couldn't have talked even if I had wanted to. He slowly lowered the dipper to me. By then I wanted the water so bad that I was ready to stand up and reach for it. Yet I held myself down on the ground waiting for the water to come to me.

I felt I earned the right for the water to come to where I was sitting. At long last the dipper was in my hands. I wanted to just guzzle it down and get some more, but I stopped myself and thought of the last three days. Then I thought of the flag pole. What if it had been all the way to the top? I still wouldn't be drinking. I thought of the spirits that had helped me so much.

I raised the dipper in gratitude, respect, to honor Grandfather and the spirits. Slowly I tipped the

dipper letting a small amount of water drip out and
splash on Mother Earth to honor her. Now I felt that
it was my turn. With shaking hands, I raised the
dipper to my mouth. That first sip was like nothing
I had ever experienced. It was heaven. I could feel
that wonderful wet trickle slowly working its way
down my dry throat. It was like putting water on a
sponge. I continued to take small sips.

After the first taste that didn't do much, I was
finally starting to make a little saliva in my mouth.
Each time I took a sip, my lips trembled. Little drops
escaped my lips. They would race down my chin,
then drop off, landing in my lap. At long last I was
feeling half way human again. Reluctantly I
surrendered the dipper. It passed on and on to the
other Sundancers until the helpers reached the end of
the line. Everyone has had their water and we started
taking our sheets down.

Earlier that morning we had given our sleeping
rolls and all other things that we didn't need to
relatives. So we didn't have much to carry out.
Finally, we lined up. The Sundance Chief held his
hand up for us to follow him.

It was finally over.

As we filed out of the Arbor, the spectators lined
up on each side of the entrance. As we walked
between them, the people reached out to touch us.
They thanked us for our prayers. Everyone was
smiling, laughing and shaking our hands. What a
wonderful feeling, I got pretty emotional. I shed a
few tears of thanks and gratefulness.

They were there, the people who had prayed and
stood by us were there until the last drum beat. They
had suffered almost as much as we had. I found out
later that many people had fasted with us. They go
without water for three days and in a way its harder
than what we had done. Because they had water,
food and other cold drinks right in front of them.

They still went without drinking.

Although not drinking, we at least did not have it around to tempt us. Its harder to resist if what you want is right there in front of you. You have no one to stop you except yourself.

Anyways, as we filed out, we felt great!

The time of suffering was over.

Lots of people wanted our Sun energy, the energy that for three days, we had pulled down onto ourselves. That energy is powerful, it's clean, heals and cures. I was so grateful to have shared the wonderful ceremony called the Sundance with the Shoshoni people.

As I was walking I felt exhilarated, I felt so good it was like walking on feathered ground. Now, I didn't feel the small sharp rocks that had made my life so interesting for the last three days. I was no longer worried about the small cactus that had for three days attacked my feet at every opportunity.

Now that the prospect of eating was close, I didn't feel the hunger. At the end of the line, I could see a large crowd ahead of me. Sundancers wrapped in white sheets, dispersed and headed in different directions, to wherever their camps were. I could see them all clutching something in their arms.

Suddenly it was my turn. A Sundance Chief's helper stood on the ground right behind a pickup truck. He was handing each Sundancer a large, striped watermelon. Oh, what an unexpected surprise. Here I had thought I didn't have any liquids left in my body. At the sight of the big, beautiful watermelon, saliva slowly moistened the whole inside of my mouth.

Again, I had received another surprise. It's amazing how little things have so much meaning. When a person has suffered and has had to do without the basic things in life, little things mean a lot. A chair to sit on, a drink of water, a small meal that's what is important in life. Even a small piece of bread becomes something to think and dream about when you are in that state.

My wife and family were all there waiting for me. My children looked like they had also been in the Sundance. They looked tired and drained. Especially two of my girls, they are twins. I believe in their innocence and because of their love for me they tried to take my pain, hunger and thirst from me. I have found out since then, in their own way, they are very powerful individuals. Especially one of them, she has always been the runt of the family. However, her energy is so strong, only my influence as her father, can keep her on the right track.

I realize that sometime I'm going to let her go, to do the things that she needs to do for the Creator. I have recognized her energy since childhood. I have also noticed her leadership qualities. If God gives me life and health, I will write about it someday.

When I saw them and felt their anxiety for me, the emotion welled up. My heart felt as though it was convulsing. "My God," I thought, "these babies have been suffering for me, as much as I have."

The enormous swelling I felt in my chest rose into my throat and brought tears to my eyes. Right then, I felt so much love for them and the whole world that I thought,

"Yes! Yes! Yes! Yes! This is what it's all about! This is why I Sundanced!"

We walked back to camp, it was a quiet and slow process. I set the pace and everyone stayed next to me. The children wanted to touch and hug me as we all walked along. This made the progress slower. There is something else I feel I must mention. The main reason I was dragging my feet was that I felt an unexplainable sense of loss. I felt an emptiness inside. As if I were leaving a part of me behind.

The only way I could try to compare this feeling,

would be to say it must be like when a woman gives birth. After giving birth, she goes through a feeling of loss, or emptiness. The Sundance is a trial and test of your spirit. It's exhilarating, yet hard. Like a woman must feel when she has a baby.

What I saw, and experienced at that first Sundance, is as close to going to the other side without making the permanent transition. I gained strength, appreciation for the basics in life and respect for all humanity.

I experienced pain, hunger and all other things that make life unpleasant and learned how to cope with it. I learned that we must consider others before we act. By not doing so we could get hurt, if we hurt others, even if done unintentionally.

As Native people, we don't always have specific words for everything. We do believe that if we do anything wrong to someone else, it comes back to us. Some people call this Karma.

Our connection with nature, our mother the earth and with the heavens, allows us to know and feel things that others overlook. It's not because of any other reason except that we have developed a sensitivity to the earth. The elements and human connections were never lost.

I believe that every living thing on this earth is born with that special sensitivity. Through no fault of our own, from childhood we learn to overlook many laws of nature. For our convenience and progress, our environment suffers.

Believe this, when nature makes up its mind, it's going to put things back where she wants them. We are not going to change nature. We have to respect nature and try to live with her. This is what we forget. Native people learned that to try to force nature to bend our way, or as we call her, Grandmother (the earth), is to look for disaster.

What I'm trying to say is that instead of trying to

be so logical, we should use a little of the common sense God gave us. Have we become so intelligent that we can't believe in the simple things? It's almost as if we follow down a road of destruction because we learn to believe only what we can see! And see only what we want to!

When the Creator formed the Earth, he had us in mind and did everything perfect and balanced. When everything was running smoothly, he created humans and already set up the food chain for the vegetables and animal world. *So why did he create us?*

The answer is hard to find, but very simple in content! We believe that when the earth was brought to life, the Creator had to think of everything.

Even before he created the animals to walk the earth, he knew that he was going to create humans and spirituality would be needed. So he had to supply a means for them to protect themselves spiritually as they were learning.

The best thing he brought us was the "mother plant." The very first plant he created was Sage. "Pejuta Wakan" as the Lakota people call it. That is the reason Sage is sacred to all traditional native people. We believe that the Creator gave it to native people to use it, in whatever way we need it. It was not to be sold in every store and by everyone.

Personally I believe that if it is sold, by anyone it should be native people who have earned the right. The Creator brought it to us so we could help ourselves, spiritually and if we had to, economically.

The Creator knew that we would need the smoke from the sage to cleanse our body and our spirits. Therefore he made different sage plants so it could survive at different altitudes and different areas. He wanted his children to have sage available to them everywhere. After Grandfather made sure we had what we needed for our spirituality, then he created humans. He made each of us different. He knew that we had to be different because he was going to give us distinguishing features from the other animals.

We have free will, creativity, intelligence, courage, integrity, resourcefulness, pride and best of all the ability to love. However, worst of all, he gave us the ability to over-emphasize our own worth. We call this ability ego! We must all learn to have respect for each other, and all other living things on this earth. We also need to learn to stop being judgemental of others. No matter how we feel, we all share this earth mother together. Whether we like it or not, we are all brothers and sisters.

When we learn these simple little things, we have taken the first step to becoming a useful part of this earth, instead of a detriment.

When we finally arrived back to camp, the women had laid out a feast on a long table. I was about the third Sundancer to arrive back to camp. The others were standing around just waiting.

My reserves and control started collapsing when I saw all that beautiful food! They prepared steaks, stew, fry bread, ice cold choke cherry juice, choke cherry pudding, coolers full of cold pop, cold watermelon, boiling hot coffee. There was so many, many wonderful things to eat. Why were we waiting? I almost lost it and embarrassed myself and started eating. Before I did I looked around and realized everyone was as hungry as I, so there was a reason for the hesitation. I looked questioningly at another Sundancer. He whispered in my ear that we were waiting for someone to do a blessing and give thanks for a good Sundance.

With that done, everybody started digging in. I didn't know what to eat first. I had a small piece of meat wrapped in a tortilla, burrito style. Then, I had a piece of watermelon. Then I asked for a cup of coffee. I never realized how good food tastes.

Ah! At last, a cigarette and a cup of hot coffee,

mingled with the smell of burning wood. There is so much to appreciate in this short life of ours.

I thought I'd have another slice of watermelon. I couldn't believe it, my stomach felt as if it was going to burst. I was so full I was hurting. My stomach had shrunken to about the size of my fist.

I found out later that I had lost twenty-five pounds, in that three days. Unfortunately, it doesn't stay off. Dehydration causes the weight loss. When you replace the fluids in your body, you are right back to where you were before. It doesn't take long.

Let me explain the reasons we go without food, or water and blow on our Eagle whistle in the Sundance. All that gets us into focusing on reaching an open and accepting state of heart and mind. This helps us become open to receive our visions.

I looked around and none of the Sundancers could finish what they had put on their plates. After eating, the atmosphere was really light. Many Sundancers started piling into cars, pickups and vans.

"Come on Manny," they yelled.

"Where's everybody going," I asked.

"We're going for a swim in the lake!"

Then somebody messed up and told me that the water was ice cold. That did it! "No thanks," I said. "I'll wait right here for you."

They left the campgrounds for two or three hours. When they returned, they were all happy, yelling and hungry again. We all ate again, soon everyone was settling down. It was starting to get toward sundown. Everyone was in great spirits and relaxing.

Then one by one each Sundancer began relating what happened to them, what they had felt, seen or experienced. It was beautiful to sit, listen and wonder where all this energy had come from, and listen to stories and the crackling of the burning wood in the campfires. It felt good to sit and stop dancing on those little sharp stones. I was glad to be smoking a cigarette, with a cup of coffee and just relaxing.

The small children started going to bed one by one. The older people just kept on talking and visiting. If you have ever sat around a campfire as the earth quiets down after a long day, you'll know what I'm talking about. It's a unique experience of feeling our mother earth as she relaxes after watching over her children all day long.

Then, as it got later, the big people also started drifting to wherever they were staying. Not everyone was camping with us. So as they left, they bid us goodbye because some were pulling out early.

Reality was back.   Lots of dancers and people who helped us while we were in, had to get back to work. Some travelled long distances and had gone to great expense to attend or help at the Sundance.

One thing that impressed me the most was, nobody was told they have to come or be at the Sundance. Dancers, helpers and everyone else are there because they want to be. Invariably the last thing everyone says is "see you next year!"

That night as I lay there trying to go to sleep, I couldn't. I kept reliving the Sundance. I had mixed feelings. I was still high from what I had received, that huge spiritual uplifting. My mixed feelings were joy, happiness at having found the Sundance. Most of all the wonder of the new world that was open to me now. I would never be the same.

I laid there so at peace with myself and my new found world that I felt as if I never closed my eyes. Suddenly, it was getting light.

In the distance I heard a couple of cars start up and quietly drive away. The drivers seemed reluctant to leave, and break the quiet spell of that sacred place. The departure of those first two cars was like a signal. From all around the Sundance grounds, I could hear people starting to talk. Car doors slammed, babies cried, and more cars left the camp. Someone in our camp put kindling on the hot coals from the night before.

It wasn't long before I started smelling coffee. I was very comfortable, but I thought of getting up. Then I wiggled my toes and they were so sore I decided to stay right where I was. Then someone started frying bacon. That was it, the very first whiff of it, and my stomach started growling. There was no denying it. I wanted something in it.

Then, of course, there is the old call of nature. I decided to get up. After everyone had eaten, we started to break camp. It took several hours to accomplish. With all that done, our foot prints and tire tracks in the dirt were all the marks that remained. Even the holes were refilled where our shade poles had been. There wasn't one tiny little piece of trash, paper or anything, anywhere. Everyone else left their camps clean.

Finally, it was time to leave. We said our goodbyes to Allen and his family. Not long after that, I went to Oklahoma on a selling trip. The native people of that state are the finest you can meet anywhere. They made me feel so welcome. I fell in love with the country around Tulsa, Oklahoma. I set up at a large native art and craft show in Telaquah and met quite a few, wonderful, Cherokee people.

Telaquah is considered the capital of the Cherokee nation. This is where all the people searching for their Cherokee roots go to find out about their heritage.

I was so taken by the people and area that when I returned to Idaho, I talked my wife into moving there.

That year went by so quickly, before I knew it, it was time to return to Wyoming for another Sundance.

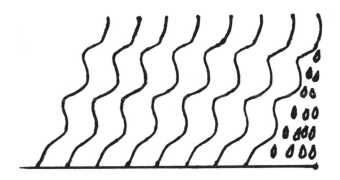

SOUTH - WHITE

"Warm Winds"
Rain

We left from Oklahoma about two weeks before the Sundance was to start. I wanted to be there with plenty of time to help with the camp and Arbor. We got set up early, but I never got to help with the Arbor. They always have plenty of young men to help do that. Get the sacred tree set up.

The erecting of the Arbor can be complicated and hard. It takes many men a long time to put it up. They've never been late. Sometimes it's as though it's not going to be done in time.

Once I really got worried because it was late afternoon and there wasn't anyone around the Arbor. I mentioned it to Allen. He just shrugged his shoulder and told me not to worry. The next time I thought about it I looked, and it was complete as though by magic.

There was still no one around, not that I could see. So, I stopped worrying about that. That was someone else's job. Our job was to do the praying and dancing.

We had plenty of time to cut brush for our camp, and dig the holes for the frame. The frame consists of whatever materials are available. Using two by fours, four by fours, teepee poles or whatever is on hand. Since it's not a permanent structure, we don't feel that what we use to make it is important. Only that it serves the purpose. You know what they say, as long as the shell covers the nut.

As the days went on, more Sundancers arrived. Some would come by and stop at our camp. We were happy to reestablish old acquaintances from the year before. One guy, Benny grinned when he saw me and asked, "Hey Manny, come back for seconds?"

Allen told me that some guys only come to the Sundance once. After being through one Sundance, they never return because of the suffering that a person goes through. It is very difficult.

At the time we heard of one guy who was riding his motor cycle to the Sundance from Western Montana. Because he thought he was going to be late, he was speeding. He got stopped. Fortunately, after taking him to jail, one police officer was Native American. The Sundancer explained why he was speeding. The officer understood and spoke for the Sundancer. He was released so he could get to the Sundance. He was lucky that he had found someone who respects the Sundance and people who take part in it. This being my second time made me an old timer. I felt welcome and proud of myself.

I guess that even if it's not supposed to be a macho thing, people still reserve judgment on how a man can act under those unusual conditions. Those people, the Shoshoni and I guess all native people, place a great deal of importance on bravery. Bravery has always been and continues to be a large and very important part of our warrior societies and our way of life. In the old days they judged you on how you endured hardships. People wanted to know if you would and could persevere, in time of hardship or trouble. Are you dependable and trustworthy? Many people believed that the Sundance is a test of manhood. Although it isn't, I believe it does border on it. Several Sundancers greeted me a little bit nicer than they had my first year.

Now that I knew what was happening, things were a little easier for me. However, there were some things they had forgotten to tell me. Like "Oh, Manny, I forgot to tell you that when you dance once, you have made a commitment to Sundance for four years."

"Oh, I forgot to tell you that once we're in the Arbor, we can't leave for any reason at all."

A person cannot leave even if he wants to. The reason it becomes impossible to leave, is that once all the Sundancers have come together, we become one entity. We become a solid power or force and as one, our power is tremendous. All our prayers will be answered. If even one person leaves the circle of a Sundance, it can cause a weakness in the rest of us. It weakens not only the dancers but also our ability to function as one and it weakens us as individuals. It's like when a person loses an arm, a leg or some part of the body. The body still lives, but the abilities become limited.

This is the reason you should know what you're getting into, from the beginning. Once in, there is no going back. If necessary, you would be kept there by force to keep from breaking the Sacred Circle. My second Sundance happened much like the first. I was feeling pretty cocky. I thought that my first one had been pretty easy. In a year you forget many things. You forget all the aches, pains, thirst and hunger.

One elder I mentioned it to, looked at me for a long time. Then he told me, "Don't be so cocky about it, and show more respect. The Spirits are there to help you, but if you take it lightly, they have ways of humbling you and making you show respect. They can make the Sundance very hard on you!"

And, did they ever!

We had gone in Friday just like before. The first night was quickly over. The drum started early next morning. We only have room for one drum at a time. They started singing and drumming, the songs were beautiful and the energy good. Everyone was happy, excited and dancing strong and hard.

We would rush at the tree and after touching it for power and energy, dance back to our spots. We were blowing furiously on our Eagle whistles the whole time. I danced without regard to my physical condition. I danced without regard to the future of my next three days. Most dancers would pace themselves so they could last the entire dance. They advised me to do the same. I didn't! My energy was so high that I just couldn't help myself.

I wanted to dance. I wanted that Sun Power on me. I wanted to feel the total glory of the Sundance. I had fallen in love with the Sundance and its beliefs.

I didn't understand it all, and I never will. Some Sundancers dance all their lives and learn more every time they dance. It's very much like an ongoing lesson in life. I knew that I had found the very best for myself. A Sundance Chief once told me that he learns something new every year.

I heard some people, for whatever reasons, will call down the Sun power on other dancers. Their object is to elevate that person with so much power and energy their dancing creates a pull of energy. It causes that dancer to have a vision right there in the Sundance. I also heard some dancers do the same thing only with malice in their hearts by calling down the Sun Power on one dancer. This causes him to dance until he drops from exhaustion. Once a dancer has reached that point of dehydration, he suffers immensely through the remainder of the Sundance. It's a very long, hard time. In a way, it's also a very cruel thing to do. Its something done to outsiders, people who don't belong there.

I don't know if that's what happened to me, but I was badly dehydrated by Saturday evening. This was only the first day. I was starting to have illusions and see things. The evening saved me. At the time I started to hallucinate it was getting late. I don't believe anyone knew what I was going through.

The day ended.

The only one who could have known how I felt was Allen. He only made a slight passing remark at how tired I looked.

Sunday morning, after greeting the Sun, everyone got ready to start dancing. Although there's only room for one drum at a time, when one group of singers tired another group took their place. There must have been five or six groups of singers.

They started singing all those beautiful Sundance songs. One song after another, such beautiful songs, every one of them. These songs stay in your mind long after a Sundance, you find yourself singing them over in your head for months. They didn't give us much time to rest.

The singers were there and eager to be singing. We had danced and danced and danced. This new day was the same as the previous morning, it got hot very early. There wasn't even the slightest breeze stirring.

It was hot! So, so hot!

I was so thirsty!

By the middle of the afternoon I started retching from my mouth being dry from dehydration. There wasn't saliva in my mouth. In its place was a gummy substance that made me sick to my stomach. I was starting to feel the effects of the day before. Combined with another night without water, it became hard to pray as my thirst took over my concentration.

In the next few hours I suffered like I never had all my life. I had gone without water for long periods before, but never like this. I can't tell you how I looked, but I can tell you how I felt.

By now hunger had ceased being a big problem. The thirst and deep dry feeling now dominated my thoughts. It started behind my eyes and into my mouth, throat and engulfed my entire body. Although the thirst centered in my mouth and throat, my arms and legs felt detached from the rest of me. It felt as if my head was floating high above me.

The feeling of it all, is almost beyond words. It's a beautiful, glorious feeling because you know why this is all happening to you. Yet, a small part of your brain questions your sanity.

"Why am I, doing this to myself?"

"Is this really worth what I'm putting myself through?"

Then thoughts of my children invaded my brain, and my friends who needed prayers, all remind me of why I made my commitment. I realize that in spite of the fatigue and fuzziness, "Yes it's worth everything I'm going through."

We are all guilty of getting ourselves into situations, that once started, we question our actions and priorities. We also have the tendency to be selfish, We ask ourselves, "What am I getting out of this?" I wonder why we must always think of ourselves first?

So you see, that is what the Sundance is all about, thinking of others before yourself. When you sacrifice yourself you are showing God and the whole world that you are willing to give of yourself so others may live better, because of your sacrifices.

The drumming and singing goes on and on. The hot sun was blazing down on us as if trying to give us as much of its heat and energy as we could take.

By now, many of us are really suffering. Some dancers are staggering. That automatically makes the drummers sing faster and harder. It also makes the songs longer. They are trying to see if any of us are on the verge of collapsing, and if we are, to keep on singing until someone does fall. It is a great honor to fall with exhaustion during the dance. It brings great honor to the Sundance, the Chief, and all the dancers. The more dancers who go into this state, the greater the honor.

As I rushed at the tree I was praying hard for my father and my mother. Each time I danced back from the tree I blew hard on my Eagle whistle. I was asking God to please answer my prayers. I had so many people to pray for, each time I danced back and forth I focused on another person.

Remember, when I first made the commitment to Sundance, I was afraid to face the unknown because of my lack of knowledge. In one of my prayers before the Sundance, I asked the Creator to help me. I asked Him to give me the courage to go through the Sundance and the strength to complete it.

If he did, I would let my hair grow long in his honor. I also promised Him that I would let it grow until my commitment was over.

"Well," my Victorian father said, "no man with long hair can come into my house." I felt rejected and hurt by my father's reactions to my choices. I didn't blame him for acting the way he did.

My parents brought us up to be humble, keep a steady job, and wear our hair short. That's what the Christian society demanded of us. So in a way I understood. My dad just didn't know any other way. I tried to tell him why I had to let it grow. He would not listen to reason. So, I explained to my mother about the Sundance and the significance of growing my hair. Although she understood, she had to stick by my dad, right or wrong.

Because of my commitment, I didn't see my

parents for five years. Every Sundance, I kept praying that my father would accept me the way I was and understand.

Backing away from the tree I staggered and danced back to my spot, I couldn't stop myself. I fell down hard. I felt my breath leave me. My head was reeling. I went into an almost hypnotic state. I could see everything going on around me, and could hear those beautiful Sundance songs. I couldn't control my arms and legs. My legs were twitching, trying to cramp. I wanted to get up and dance some more, but I couldn't will my legs to move. It was a frightening feeling. I had my bedding rolled up in my spot just behind me. As I tried to get up, my legs just stretched out in front of me.

Allen had gone out to the Sacred tree and as he danced back I saw him stagger. When he was back all the way, he stopped, and looked at me with a question on his face. He didn't say anything. He just looked and understood that now I was going through a very personal thing.

I didn't know it myself, but I was going through a very real vision. The hunger, the thirst and the heat were combining their energy to put me in contact with the Great Spirit. Now I knew he was giving me his undivided attention. In essence, he was letting me know, that moment was mine. He had listened to my prayers. Since I was willing to sacrifice, he was willing to answer my prayers. Now he was also going to let me know about my future. This was the moment when I was going to receive direction for my life. It would be done through my vision, as interpreted by an elder.

My vision came.

My world, my eyesight, everything as I knew it went blank! Suddenly, everything came into focus, but, seemed so unreal. I could see the green leaves of the Arbor brush. The color was so bright, so green, they almost gave off light. The sky was an intense blue. Everything I looked at was vibrant and in clear, sharp detail.

The sun was very, very bright, but it was no longer hot. It didn't bother me in any way. It felt so pleasant, I just wanted to sleep. I was the only one in the Arbor. All the other dancers disappeared. There was no more drumming or singing. It was absolutely still. I was laying just north of the Sacred tree, with my feet pointing toward it. My eyes closed, yet I could see all those things.

Suddenly, I heard a loud, flapping noise. I opened my eyes and there between the poles in the roof of the Arbor, I saw a huge Spotted Eagle descending into the Arbor.

He was so big I knew he couldn't possibly get through between the rafters. The rafters were invisible to the Eagle. He flew right through them as though they didn't exist. He soared right to where I was laying, and landed lightly on my chest.

I couldn't move, my body rigid with fright. I felt the pressure of his weight on my chest. I could smell his feathers that were hot from the sun. I could feel the warmth of his body.

As the Eagle stood on my chest, in slow motion, he looked down and right into my eyes. We made eye contact. I could see very clearly the golden flakes in the iris of his eyes. I tried to read a message or something. I couldn't, but, I got a distinct intuition that I didn't have to be afraid.

I felt myself relax, and as I did each of his talons slowly gripped my chest. Slowly, the talons, one by one pierced my skin and dug into my flesh.

I flinched, expecting pain, but surprisingly, felt

only the popping sensation as each talon broke through my flesh. As I lay there, the Eagle still looked right into my eyes.

His look said, "I told you not to be afraid and it would not hurt!"

So, I lay there, held my breath, and waited to see what was going to happen.

The Eagle slowly spread its magnificent wings, and ever so slowly, started flapping them. I could smell and taste the dust disturbed by its wings. In two or three huge flaps we were off the Arbor floor. As we lifted off, the Eagle seemed slow because of my weight.

About this time I felt my spirit separate from my vision. It was as though I was leaving my vision to become an observer. The Eagle had told me, in his way that he was going to take me up to show me where I could help others.

The Eagle spirit and myself soared high above the ground, so high I could see the curvature of our Mother Earth. He was showing me that I would be helping people in all directions, and that I would be ready when the time was right. I would be told and shown the way to help people, by a Medicine Man.

I could see my vision below me, the Eagle and my body, as he was flapping between the ground and the rafters. I realized that I had split into three separate entities of myself! My physical body on the ground, my spirit being pulled by the Eagle's talons and my soul was watching the entire scene!

As we soared higher, I felt fear, but only because of nothing to hold onto. My soul seemed suspended next to the Eagle spirit as he talked to me through thought. Suddenly, I was back in my vision. Again I could feel the wind stirred up by the Eagle's wings.

We moved past the rafters, and realization hit me. I was being taken from the Sundance! My thoughts screamed, "I don't want to leave this Arbor. I'm not done with my Sundance!"

Boldly, I grabbed for the rafters and yelled at the Eagle to let me down that I didn't want to break the circle. I reached out with both arms and grabbed a rafter. When I grabbed the rafter, I felt the pain in my chest where the Eagle's talons had pierced my flesh. The Spotted Eagle kept flapping his wings hard, then harder and stronger. It was as if he was trying to break my grip off the rafter. Desperately, I hung on. His huge wings were so powerful, for a moment, I felt like just letting go. Then I felt the power of our Sundance, and the importance of not breaking the Sacred Circle, so I hung on. I can still feel the wind and turbulence of his wings.

Suddenly, first one then another of his talons started ripping out of my chest.

I felt the pain then. It was a good pain because I knew that I was not to leave the Sundance.

I was not going to break the Sacred Circle. As the last talon ripped out of my flesh, my grip of the rafter finally broke. I landed softly back on the floor of the Arbor.

As I woke up from my vision I was still next to my bedroll. I opened my eyes and looked around. Everything was the same as before. The drummers were still singing, the Sundancers were dancing and going to the Sacred Tree. I wondered how true that had all been.

Had it only been a dream?

Had it only been thoughts going through my mind or hallucinations?

I really wasn't sure what had happened. All I knew was that it was real, very real. So real that I

still felt pain on both sides of my chest, above my
breast. I felt as if the Eagle's talons had virtually torn
out my flesh. It was so real, I looked down and
touched my chest to see if I was bleeding.

I staggered, I had to get on my knees and stand
up. I stood swaying and wondering if I would fall. I
felt confused as I stood there looking around.
Everything was back to normal. Nobody seemed to
have noticed a thing that had happened to me.

It had been so real that I just knew everyone else
had seen and felt what I did. It took me a few
minutes standing there to clear my mind and come
back to reality.

As I stood there shaking my head, I looked at the
tree. I could feel an intense energy coming to me
from it. It was almost like magic, the tree was
helping me and giving me strength to continue. I put
my Eagle whistle back in my mouth, and got up to
my station. There were two small trees, freshly cut
and placed between each dancer. I got up and felt a
coolness come to me from those trees, with the bark
removed. They were moist and damp.

By now we were all dry, we accepted gratefully,
the feel of moisture from those beautiful small trees.
It was so beautiful to feel dampness on our parched
skin.

The singers were still drumming and singing.

I put my Eagle whistle in my mouth and rushed
at the tree. When I got to the tree, I embraced it, and
asked Grandfather to give me strength, and direction.
I thanked him for what he had given me and for what
he had chosen to let me see. I still didn't realize that
it was a vision.

I danced back to my spot, and blew furiously on
my Eagle whistle. I couldn't believe it. I felt like I
was getting drops of moisture back into my mouth

from my Eagle whistle. It was wetting the inside of my mouth at first, then I felt my throat moisten. I was getting help from the Creator and strength and courage needed to survive this very hard Sundance.

The elder had warned me to be careful, and that some dances were harder than others. This was proving to be a harder Sundance. It was overwhelming, almost more than I could take, but I feel it was also a test by the Creator. As though he was telling me, "You had an easy one. Now try a hard one."

Suddenly, I felt so good now that I had that little bit of moisture in my mouth and my throat. I felt happy. I started looking around at my brother Sundancers and thinking, "I'm going to make it."

This is it, I have had the sign that tells me I am going to finish the Sundance. I was looking at everyone and seeing that they were going through difficulties. They dehydrated and suffered.

I started praying for them saying, "Grandfather, help my brothers." It was almost like electricity. Slowly the whole Sundance seemed to start picking up, and getting more life into it.

Even the singers and the drummers perked up. They looked around. The energy changed. It was so beautiful that everyone felt happy. Guys looked better and it was getting toward evening. It also started getting cooler.

Maybe that had something to do with it. The dance continued. I had no problems after that continuing my dancing. Late that evening, as everything finished, the drummers went back to camp. We finished for the day.

Tired from the long, hot day, the Sundancers laid down and rested. This was Sunday night. We knew that the hardest part of the Sundance was over, the longest day. We knew the next day we would be getting out. Everything was right.

I laid there thinking. Thanking the Creator for helping me, as he did in that one special moment. I got up from my bedroll I walked to where the Sundance Chief was. He was sitting on the West side of the Arbor. As is tradition when seeking counsel, I brought him some tobacco.

I shook his hand, sat and said, "I want to share something with you. I need some guidance from you."

He asked, "What do you need?"

He didn't even know my name because so many Sundancers come and go every year that he can't keep track.

I told him what had happened to me that day, how I had suffered. In a way, I wish it had happened in the middle of the Arbor so everybody would have known about it.

He said, "That's okay, it was only supposed to happen to you, it's your vision. My interpretation is there are other Sundances. The Lakota people pierce their chest, I think the spirits were telling you that you have to do that some day. Also that you are to help heal others, no matter who they are. But not yet, not until you are ready."

I asked, "Why do they bring the vision to me here?"

He explained, "Because that was one time that your mind, body and spirit are ready and open to receive this message. So it came to you in a very sacred place. Then you would know that it was real and not just your imagination. It wasn't just a dream, or just a thought. This did happen to you, this is how we get our visions."

He answered my questions and I'm not afraid to

tell you, that it scared me to death! Just the thought of piercing made me ache all over.

I thought, "My God, I can't do that."

However, that was his answer. That was his interpretation of my vision.

I asked him one final thing, "When do I have to do this?"

He said, "When you are at the Sundance the first time, you make a four year commitment. The reason the spirits demand this is so that they can see that we are sincere in following the Sundance spirituality and traditions. You must go to the Lakota Sundance, and pierce as your vision told you, but first you must finish your four years with the Shoshoni people."

After receiving the interpretation of my vision, I returned to my bedroll and lay down. Everybody was starting to get into their blankets because the weather was starting to get a little cool.

I lay quiet for awhile, just listening to the sounds. By the center of the Arbor the guards started their fire and kept it going all night. As I drifted off to sleep my mind was full of wonder at what had happened. I couldn't believe my mouth had saliva. It was no longer dry like it had been for two days. The last thing I recall was looking through the branches of the Arbor leaves, at the stars.

The next thing I knew, I woke about one or two o'clock in the morning. It was cold and the wind was blowing very hard. We got hit by a big storm that night. It was almost like an answer to all of our prayers. We couldn't touch or allow any water to touch our lips or go into our mouths, but we could feel the humidity in the air. When you're parched like we were, moisture can be absorbed through the skin.

Many people said at the Sundance, don't let

water touch you in any way. They meant even on the arms, hands or the face when it rains. It just makes your body cry out for more moisture. When it doesn't get it, the suffering is twice as hard as it was before.

It was cold, windy and stormy all night. We had quite a bit of rain, but by morning it was clear. This was Monday morning, now we all got up to put on the best shawl skirt that we have.

We put on our finery because we want to look good. We want to show that, although it was hard on us, we're proud of what we have done and the suffering we endured. Proud to be allowed the privilege to pray for other people.

The Creator has seen fit to let us survive, to live and talk about what we experienced. We know we have done our little bit. Everybody got ready, and greeted the sun. We always get up before the sun rises, to greet it and allow its warmth into our hearts.

The dancing went on for the remainder of the morning. Finally we concluded the Sundance that Monday afternoon about one o'clock. It was the same procedure as we left the Arbor.

We got our watermelon, people thanked and greeted us. It was such a joyous occasion. It felt as if every breath we took, every second of thirst we suffered, was all worthwhile. Simply by the gratitude shown by the people who wait for us to leave the Arbor.

In preparing the Arbor, some people go through much hardship and very hard work. They keep us going with their support. They cook for and feed the drummers and singers. There is so much to do, that it's almost easier to be inside the Arbor dancing than to be outside.

Now I'd like to tell you something about the

Sundance Chief. Four days before the Sundance, called purification days, the Sundance Chief has one full week of fasting. He allows himself a very small amount of liquids, but never water. They can be a cup of coffee or tea, but never water in its pure state. For a full week before, the Sundance Chief is already suffering. He suffers and fasts and does without water, with us, for three and four days during the Sundance. Then for four days after the Sundance, he is praying and giving thanks for all we received.

Tuesday morning I got up and went outside. I saw that lonely figure standing out there in the middle of the desert. He raised his pipe and arms to the Great Spirit, the east and the rising sun.

It was such a beautiful ceremony, but it is not for the weakhearted nor the timid. It takes courage to be a Sundance Chief, to commit yourself to that sacrifice. It's not easy. Anybody who sacrifices for another should be respected, and helped in any way possible.

This is the thing that has bothered me, the Sundance only lasts for a week. We need the spirituality the rest of the year. Then we return to reality. There should be some way that we can continue to practice our spiritual beliefs.

My family and I returned to Oklahoma. We continued our daily quest for our livelihood.

Early the next summer, we left Oklahoma so that we could go to some Pow Wows before the Sundance. We attended a couple of small Pow Wows in Colorado. Then moved on to New Mexico. We went to Taos to see some acquaintances.

We had been there a few days when Carpio, a friend we were staying with, asked me to drive his car down to Santa Fe. They were having auditions for extras, for the mini-series, "Gambler III" with

Kenny Rogers. To make the story short, although reluctant at first, my whole family ended up as extras on the set. I played a Sioux Chief.

Before the shooting of the film started, I asked Kenny Rogers' brother, Leland, if they wanted to have a Sweat Lodge with us. After agreeing to it, we built it right on the movie grounds. There were several of us with Kenny Rogers, his brother Leland, the producer Ken Kragen, and the director Dick Lowry. It was a good Sweat, Kenny was surprised at how long we were in it.

It was fun sweating with people who were new to the Sweat Lodge, they were great. It was here I met Larry, a Sundancer from Rosebud, South Dakota. Immediately after the segment I was there for, we left for the Sundance.

We went through the same thing. Preparing our Eagle whistles and getting our ceremonial outfits ready. Of course it was always good to see the people at the Sundance, they became very important, good friends to us.

The Sundancers greeted me more enthusiastically than they had my first and second years. They made me feel like I was one of them now. The days passed as the Sundance came and went. This Sundance wasn't quite as hard as my second one, but it was still hard. Everyone suffered quite a bit. Thirst was again a major factor in my suffering.

I always prayed for my family, my wife and children. I especially prayed for my father and mother that their health would last and they would be well. Also that my father would come to accept me with my long hair.

Sunday I saw something that almost caused me to have a nervous breakdown. In retrospect I believe it was indeed a spiritual breakdown. I've given this a tremendous amount of thought, whether to include it in this book. I believe it's important enough that it has to be told.

There were two lessons learned here for me, important ones. It showed me that no matter how deeply embedded in spirituality anyone is, the fact remains that we are still scared, lonely and weak human beings. The other lesson I learned is that no man should be put up on a pedestal, no one man is above reproach. If you put someone up on a pedestal, they will surely fall some day. This has been demonstrated, repeatedly with religious and spiritual leaders. Perhaps the Creator is showing us to rely on ourselves and him only.

It all began when the drummers were taking their noon break. We only had one group singing for us. As I was laying on my bedroll resting, the man next to me was one that I had looked up to and respected since I had met him. Though he was younger than me, he had been around the Sundance all his life. So in my book, that made him pretty special. At the time he wasn't married long but they had a small baby. His wife was Cheyenne.

Most of us were just laying down, resting. Some guys were asleep. Right outside the Arbor, his wife was sitting holding the baby. My wife was sitting in her chair just beyond me. In the guise of showing him the baby, underneath the baby's blanket, I saw her hand him the baby's bottle full of water. I saw this man put the nipple of the bottle in his mouth and start sucking on it.

I was shocked at what I was seeing. I turned and looked at my wife. She also had a shocked look on her face. I asked her, "Did you just see what I saw?" She nodded her head. She couldn't say anything. I then asked him "What in the world are you doing, man?" Although I tried, I couldn't quite keep the anger out of my voice.

He tried to be casual about it and said, "oh it's okay, I'm just rinsing my mouth out."

Angrily I retorted, "If its alright why don't they let all of us do that?"

"Its okay, its okay, Manny," he said trying to calm me. He didn't want anyone else to know what I had seen.

It devastated me. All I could think of was, again I'm being let down hard. Maybe I just demand too much from others. Maybe I expect too much. I'm not very tolerant when a word is given. I'm not one to forgive going back on a man's word.

He immediately returned the bottle to his wife. My wife was livid, as she also took the Sundance very seriously. She told his wife to take the baby back to camp and not bring water to the Arbor ever again. His wife got up and almost ran from the Arbor. She knew they did something sacrilegious. They also knew that it wasn't a secret any longer. Someone had seen what they had done. I turned my back to him and didn't even want to see his face. I was deeply hurt by what he had done.

Now thinking back, I wonder if I were being too judgemental, or had judged him too harshly. Did I have the right to judge him at all? He didn't hurt me, he only hurt himself. I think most of my anger was because he used an innocent child to cheat. The break down didn't happen until the next day, when I had all night to think about it. After the Sun greeting ceremony next day, I called Allen aside and told him what I saw. He couldn't believe it either.

During the telling, a combination of hunger, thirst, fatigue and emotion surged through me. The result was devastating. I was very distraught and heavily disappointed, I even tried to give away my pipe. It's hard to write what I felt, how hopeless everything looked because of one man's actions. I was crying in front of my brother Allen and couldn't seem to control myself.

This is when I believe I had my spiritual breakdown. He understood and waited patiently until my grief had expended itself. For days afterwards, I felt empty and cheated.

At the end of the Sundance, something else very dramatic happened to me. As I was coming out, we're all happy, tired, and hungry. We're very thirsty, and the people are standing outside, greeting us and shaking our hands. While walking up, I looked to my right. Just beyond the people sitting in front, was an older woman sitting. Our eyes made contact. I just smiled, nodded my head and went on.

I was elated to be getting out. It had been a hard Sundance, but not like the second one. When I got to the end of the line, they handed me a watermelon. I turned left, a young man came and touched my right shoulder. He said, "Excuse me, sir. Would you pray for my Mom?" He had mumbled the request.

I couldn't hear him too well because there was so much noise. People were talking to each other and laughing and congratulating the Sundancers. I wasn't feeling normal yet. I frowned and looked at him. I said, "I am sorry, what did you say? My throat is very dry." I could hardly speak.

Again, he repeated, "My Mom wants to know if you will pray for her."

It took a second for me to figure out what he was saying. I asked, "Why me?"

"She wants you to pray for her, no one else."

"I'm just a Sundancer, I'm not a medicine man," I said lightly.

"That's okay," he went on. "She wants you, no one else to pray for her."

"I would be honored, if she thinks I'm the right person."

"Yes, you are the one she wants."

I turned around, handed my wife the watermelon and said, "I will be right back."

I went with him to his mother, she was sitting down. She had the most beautiful face, a very wise looking face. She had long grey hair, and was so regal, so elegant, you could have sworn she was in the courts of Europe.

To be so honored in this way to pray for one of our elders, is an honor beyond description. I was close to tears. I knelt down before her, and I looked in her eyes. I asked quietly, "Grandmother, am I the one you called for? I'm not a medicine man. I'm just a Sundancer."

"Yes, I want you to pray for me, son. I feel that you can do something to help me."

"Please tell me how can I help you?"

She explained, "I have arthritis throughout my body so bad I can hardly walk. I can't walk without a cane or someone helping me. If you could just bring me a little relief from the pain I will be grateful." So, I put my hand on her right knee, and I grabbed hold of both her hands with my left hand, and I started praying. I don't recall what I said. I know that I was praying so hard that tears came to my eyes. I tried with all my energies within me. I don't know what to call it, it could have been a personal contact with God, maybe.

She might have thought that I was able to do more than just a prayer. I prayed for her. I guess I prayed for two or three minutes. As I stood up, I said, "Grandmother, I feel very inadequate in doing what you ask of me. I have done the best I can. I know it wasn't very long, but I'm tired and very thirsty."

With relief on her face, she said, "That is all I wanted, was for you to touch me and say a little prayer."

"Before I leave," I told her, "I want you to understand one thing. Although this prayer was short, I am not through praying for you. For the next four days no matter where I am, I will pray for you. I will pray that you receive help."

"That's all I want," she said gratefully, "thank you."

As I turned to leave, I touched her shoulder and walked to where my family was waiting. On our way back to camp, my wife asked me, "What did she want?"

I said, "Just a prayer. That's all she wanted was a prayer and a little relief from her pain."

I felt very humbled by the experience. She had chosen me out of seventy-five other Sundancers. To me that was a great honor.

We rested around camp, and ate. Of course my main thing was getting a slice of that watermelon.

We left the next day, and stopped at a K.O.A. campground in Casper, Wyoming.

That night I went out by myself away from all the other people camped there, and prayed for her.

I never knew her name, that beautiful lady, I've never forgotten her or her energy and face. I wish now I had asked her name, or to know her children, her grandchildren. I went and prayed, for some reason it was so intense I cried for her again.

Now I stop and look back at that. It seems this was a test for me. Perhaps she was a member of the "Bird Tribe" or an "Angel." If she was I think her mission was to show me I was ready now to help people. In helping her, it gave me confidence in my ability to help others. I believe that through her, Grandfather was showing me how close I was to my vision coming true.

Though I was tired, thirsty and wanting to eat the watermelon in my hand. Would I give that pleasure up, to help someone unknown to me? If it was a test I suppose I passed it. For when I searched for her, while walking away, I turned to look and the woman and her son had vanished. It still puzzles me to this day.

The following morning we left, as we travelled toward South Dakota. I'm not sure why we headed in that direction, we were just going. I kept listening on the radio about tornadoes here and there. Where they were going, and we were looking at the map figuring out where they were from us. One crossed in front, and one crossed behind us. We got to this little town called Valentine, Nebraska. There that evening while we were camping at a trailer park, I went out.

While I was praying for her, a big thunderstorm came. For some reason, when I prayed for her, I became emotional again, maybe because I was so fresh out of the Sundance. There was thunder, lightening and hail, so I had to cut the prayer short. It was still very good.

We left there the following morning and went through Mission, South Dakota, and the Rosebud Reservation. At the time, I never knew what my connection might be to that area, or what pulled me there. We went through the village of Parmalee, South Dakota and stopped at this little store, way out of the way. I don't know why I asked the owner, "Are there any Sundances going on around here?"

He said, "Yes. There is one going on." He

proceeded to give me directions.

However, at the time my wife said she wasn't ready for another Sundance so soon after the last one. So, I let her talk me out of it. I'm not going to put the blame on her. I'm not getting any younger, and the Sundance wore me out. That summer before the Sundance, we looked around and found a house in southwestern Colorado. We put a down payment on it and told them we'd be back later after the Sundance.

Not long after that my son, Manny, and I made a sales trip up around Jackson Hole, Wyoming. Back up through Fort Washakie, Wyoming, where the Sundance took place. We made a swing back over toward Denver, Colorado. Before we got to Denver, I got very, very sick.

I had to let my son drive. He drove most of the night into the next morning. I was very sick. I was having a hard time getting up, waking up and getting going. We went to the convention center where they were having a native art and craft show.

We went in there and I got a booth. We set up our arts and crafts to do some retailing, and while we were in this show, I almost fell down twice. I didn't know what was going on. I felt sick and thought maybe I was just hungry. Then I thought that it couldn't be hunger, I had eaten plenty.

After the second time, I almost fell out of the chair. My son said, "Hey, I don't care if I have to carry you, Dad, you are going to the hospital."

"Okay, let's go and talk to the nurse here."

They had a male nurse there at the show. The nurse asked, "What's the problem?"

I said, "I think I've had a heart attack."

The guy went haywire. He was in worse shape than I was. He started to shake and say, "Ah, ah, ah,

ah . . . I better call 911 . . . uh . . . the ambulance."
He looked around frantically. He couldn't find the
phone and all the time it was sitting right next to
him.

Finally I said, "Hey, take it easy guy, I'm not
dead yet! By the way, the phone's sitting right there
on the desk."

As sick as I felt, it was still comical watching his
reaction to the situation. He finally got an ambulance
for me. When they got me in it, they checked me
out, put me on an I.V. and sped me to the hospital.
They were still checking me out, as the ambulance
raced through the traffic. At the hospital, they put me
on that cardiovascular receiver, or whatever they call
it, they found out that I had two minor strokes within
an hour. I didn't even know what was going on.

I thought it was just bad dizzy spells. Then they
told me, when I got back home, to check with my
doctor to see what was wrong.

At the time, I didn't even have a family doctor.
So, I just went to this one doctor there in Durango.
He told me my biggest problem was I had serious
high blood pressure. From what I understand it
affects some people at high altitudes. Here we had
just bought a house two or three months before that
sits over 8,000 feet! There I was staggering around,
I couldn't do anything. I was almost totally unable to
function at home.

So, I told my wife and kids, I can't handle this.
I've got to move to a lower altitude. So we moved
back to Oklahoma.

We went right back to the little town of Inola
and found a house to rent. The following summer I
got sick and couldn't make it to the Sundance. It
wasn't just the sickness, the high blood pressure as
well. I was always in contact with Allen. He called

me and said they had changed and moved the Sundance grounds.

Allen told me they moved it from up there on the mesa, where I had been Sundancing for three years. They have changed it back to downtown Fort Washakie. He continued, "I'm not going to Sundance this year. I don't like that place. Too many drunks come around yelling obscenities at us and stuff. It's not a good place for a Sundance. So I won't be going."

"Well, I've been sick Allen, so I am going to have to miss this year," I explained.

Throughout all this sickness, with everything I had gone through, I felt empty not going to the Sundance. As though a big piece of my life had been cut out. Yet I knew that healthwise I wasn't ready, also the location wasn't good for me. So, I thought, this is the way it's supposed to be. That year would have been my fourth year.

The following year, I went to California to see some friends of mine, Wolfhawk, Steve and Chrys. I had met them during the movie shoot in Santa Fe. I also met Larry, who Sundanced in Rosebud. When I had missed my fourth year with the Shoshoni, all I wanted was to finish my commitment.

In my mind I couldn't picture myself going back to the Sundance if I had to sit and listen to drunks and other people who didn't believe our way. So by now I figured that I wasn't going back to the Shoshoni Sundance. I asked Larry if I could finish my fourth Sundance with them in Rosebud.

He said, "Of course you can, Manny. You're more than welcome to come with us. We'll help you any way that we can."

Now here it was, three weeks before the Shoshoni Sundance. The phone rings, and it was

Allen.

I said "What's going on?"

He said "The Sundance is back on, bud. It's back on the Mesa where you danced your first three years." He was very enthusiastic and happy, "You're going to love it, it's really going to be a good one this year."

I groaned, "Oh my God, I already committed this summer to the Rosebud Sundance with Larry." I explained everything to Allen. He seemed crestfallen, but told me to do what I had to do.

Now I was sick to my stomach. I really didn't know what to do. The Shoshoni people honored me by allowing me to dance with them. I couldn't let them down. So I told Allen, "I'll be there."

He said "Okay."

When I told my wife that it was back on in Wyoming, she said, "What are you going to do about South Dakota?"

I said "Well, we'll go to the Shoshoni, and I'll dance there. Then we'll go to South Dakota, and tell Larry that I've already finished my four years."

She said, "Well that sounds okay to me. He won't hold you to it."

"I don't think so either. I think he's pretty understanding."

So, that year we went. We prepared just like the other three years.

Incidentally, when you make a commitment for four years, nothing says you have to do them consecutively. The agreement with the Creator is to dance four years. If it takes you six years to finish four years, that's fine, just so you finish them.

We went there, we prepared, I Sundanced, and it was a very hard one. I want to point out that I hardly ever mention hunger. Hunger is not a factor.

When you get so dry you forget everything else. What really becomes prominent is your thirst. The hunger you can live with. You can go several days without eating. Although, the first twenty-four hours without food can be the hardest, after that it gets easier. So, we went through the Sundance. Other than it being hard, and losing another twenty-five pounds from lack of moisture, it was a good Sundance, and a beautiful one.

There's nothing common about any Sundance, they have all got their special things that happen when you're in there. Although it would be hard to top my second and third Sundances, because of my vision, and somebody asking me to pray for them, it was really special. To be chosen from seventy-five other Sundancers was quite an honor.

We got through with the Sundance, and said our farewells to all our friends. Before the Sundance was over, I had bought some things, and honored the drum. I was giving thanks. That was my give-away, I had to have a give-away because it was my fourth Sundance and I was finishing my commitment.

I honored many of my friends who I had danced with for four years, had encouraged me, and gave me strength or energy to get through rough spots. I honored Allen, Benny, Edgar - the Sundance Chief and most of all I thanked and honored the Creator. I asked him to look after my family, I was deeply grateful to Him for helping me these four years.

We drove north then across over to Rapid City. We ended up in Mission, South Dakota. We got a few groceries there and tried to find Larry. I already had directions. We went to where his stepmother lived and found him.

Grinning he said, "You're sure here early. The Sundance isn't until this coming weekend."

I explained cautiously, "Larry we just came by to tell you that I can't do the Sundance. I have already finished my four years. They called me and told me that the Shoshoni Sundance was on again. That's where we are coming from."

"That's okay, Manny. I appreciate you coming by and letting me know, instead of just not showing up. No, you've got no obligation except to yourself. If that satisfies you, that should be good enough for everybody else."

I didn't know what he meant at the time, although it dawned on me later.

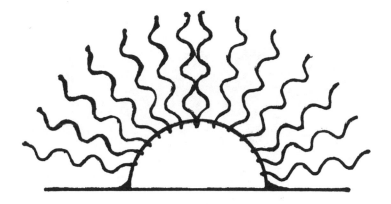

WEST - BLACK

"Setting Sun"
Day's End

We were only there at Larry's house, ten, maybe fifteen minutes. We left and headed back to Oklahoma. As we travelled, there was almost an eerie silence in the van. When I had told Larry that I wasn't going to be dancing with them, I felt an emptiness inside. I couldn't explain it. Then I got to thinking about what he had said to me.

"If you are happy with the commitment you have made and what you are doing now. If that satisfies you, that's good enough for everybody."

Except what he didn't say was that I had made that commitment to the Creator. There was always that thought in the back of my mind about my vision. It had been so vivid. I couldn't just forget it.

I kept remembering my vision. I realized that my commitment had been made for me by my vision, yet we kept travelling south. At the time my wife discouraged me from going. I didn't know why.

While looking for Larry, we happened to go by another Sundance because we heard he might be there. When we stopped we saw men dancing and piercing. It frightened my wife, the whole ceremony scared her badly. She wouldn't even get out of the van. She could see through the bushes in the camp, and into the Arbor. This was also the first time I had seen it. I was glad I'd finished my four years! Frankly, the whole scene scared me too. I believe, although she would never admit it, she was deathly afraid of the piercing ceremony, even just seeing it.

We headed all the way back to Oklahoma, getting there Sunday evening. When we got home, I knew this was the time the Rosebud Sundancers were going through purification. The actual Sundance didn't start until the following Thursday.

Monday morning I worked in our little shop all day. No matter how hard I worked I couldn't tear the thought from my mind that I wasn't completing my commitment and was abandoning the Creator. Although my promise was made under unusual circumstances, that is what Larry meant. I said I'd be there, and the Creator wasn't going to let me forget it easily. He was going to make me uncomfortable, I guess. I don't know . . . actually, I was making myself uncomfortable.

Tuesday morning I got up and I worked again all day, making crafts. I was making lances, war clubs. I was doing war shields trying to get the thought of the Sundance out of my mind. Most of the time I was at the shop, I was there by myself. My kids were already in school by then.

I was spending some time by myself. The next morning I couldn't handle it anymore. I was sitting watching CNN, to see what had happened the night before while I was asleep when my wife walked in and said good morning.

I said, "I'm going to the Sundance."

She said, "I knew it, I could feel it. I'm surprised you waited until Wednesday, I thought you were leaving Monday morning. I've got your suitcase all packed. I fixed you some sandwiches after you went to bed, so, you are all ready to go."

"I am really sorry I am spending this time and this money going."

She said, "You know you have to go."

So, she knew about my commitment, she just didn't want any part of it, and I can't blame her for it either. In a way because it is something alien to many people. They find it really hard to accept. Seeing other human beings suffering like this, but that's all part of our prayers.

So I left. I drove through Oklahoma, Kansas,

Nebraska, until I finally got about ninety miles outside South Dakota. I just couldn't go any more. It was one in the morning, and I was beat. I started to fall asleep at the wheel, so I stopped and slept about five or six hours.

Next morning, when I arrived, they were already in the Sundance. Heart broken because I had tried so hard to make it, I found Larry. I suppose that wasn't to be my first day. Everyone greeted me and made me feel welcome. My friend Steve's sister, Chrys, and I walked to the Arbor. I saw Larry and Steve, and they were happy to see me.

Larry said, "You came back, did you?"

"I had to, Larry."

With a knowing smile on his face, he nodded his head. As though he knew I would be there, but had to find out myself. He couldn't tell me to stay. I read so much in the look that he gave me.

He said, "Look Manny, get yourself together, get some rest today because it isn't easy. It's really hard. You can come in tomorrow morning."

"I could use some rest," I said gratefully.

When I got back to camp the girls told me what I needed. A head crown of sage wrapped in cloth, ankle and wrist bands in the same material, and a skirt. They helped me get it together and went out and got some long stems of sage for me.

The next morning I laid there for the longest time, wide awake. I was anxious to get going into this new Sundance the Creator was showing me. I felt excited and nervous. I don't know how much I slept that night, but it couldn't have been a lot.

Then I heard somebody call over a P.A. system.

"Alright, Sundancers . . . Sundancers, time to get up, time to get going. The Sweat Lodges are ready."

My stomach lurched. Butterflies were having a

good old time in my stomach. This was it. I jumped up and went over to Steve's tent and called him. He got up, and we put our towels around us, and headed to the Sweat Lodges. It is a special feeling to be up that early in the morning for such a special occasion. We walked over barefoot.

This Sundance is a lot different from the other. They had four Sweat Lodges behind the Arbor, and the fire pit was going. The flames were high. There were several people starting to gather. In the Lakota Sundance, we have to purify every day before we go into the sacred Arbor. Then we purify every night after coming out. This is part of the ceremony.

Steve and I walked up together where the Sweat Lodges were. I had a little tingling sensation at the pit of my stomach. I felt apprehensive, a little nervous, a little scared. So many things were going through my mind. This was the result of the vision that I had two or three years before. So here I was, excited, nervous or a combination of both. It was a very pleasant, unusual sensation.

The morning was pretty cool as we walked up to the Sweat Lodges. The first thing I felt was the heat from the big fire. It was warm and friendly and seemed to wash my apprehension from me. Not only did the fire have a calming, soothing effect on me, it seemed to relax everyone else. There is something very special about the fires that are heating up the Stone People for the Sweat Lodges, getting them ready to bring us their breath. We would have our bodies, minds, spirits, and energies purified by them. As we walked up, from out of the Sweat Lodges, we heard someone call. The faint and muffled voice from the Sweat Lodge said, "Come on in, we've got room for two more."

So, Steve got down on his hands and knees and I followed. We crawled into the Sweat Lodge. When entering any Lakota Sweat Lodge a person always says the words "*Mitakuye Oyasin,*" which means "all my relations." A very loose interpretation is that you're asking the spirits to cover all the people of the world in your prayers. We believe we are all related. The Sundance colors are red, yellow, white and black. The four races, we are all one people.

When we got in the Sweat Lodge the leader called out, "Alright, bring me seven rocks, seven Grandfather rocks." By that, he meant he wanted some pretty good size rocks. The fire keeper went over and got the first rock. With the pitch fork he brought it over. As he brought it into the Sweat Lodge, the leader guided it into a special spot, and placed in the small hole in the center. They repeated the process seven times. As they brought each rock in, one Sundancer sprinkled a few pieces of cedar on top of the hot rocks.

Right away they started popping and sending out a beautiful, rich scent of cedar into the Sweat Lodge. All of us were sitting there, waiting solemnly. The Sweat Lodge is a very important ceremony in our culture. Anyone who has been in one knows how close you are to the other people. Almost immediately after the first stone was in, the sweat started beading up on my forehead. It trickled down my neck and back. It was so pleasant, and felt really good, after coming in from the outside that was cool.

Anyways, when the final stone was in place, they brought in a bucket of water. We asked a blessing for it from the Grandfather rocks. Then we closed the door flap, plunging us into total darkness. We never discuss what we hear or talk about in the Sweat Lodge, on the outside. We believe once a problem is spoken of in the Sweat Lodge, it is to be left there. If someone discusses anything heard in the Sweat Lodge, when they go outside, we believe it returns to the person talking about it. The whole purpose of the Sweat Lodge is to leave all your problems in there, and to ask for blessings on all our relatives.

However, we do give thanks that we were all at the Sundance, and we ask for strength and the courage to go through it. All I could think of was the sensation I had, in my second Sundance, when I had my vision. My chest, even now after three years, was starting to itch again. I admit that I felt a little bit of dread. Also scared, not knowing how I was going to react or that I might fail. In retrospect, I suppose everyone goes through that.

It was a quick, one round sweat that is typical. It's traditional in the Lakota Sundance. Sometimes they can get pretty hot. Most of the time the Sundance leaders are the ones that run the "*Inipi*" or Sweat Lodge ceremony. There are others who run them, depending on availability. They are pretty considerate of the dancers, and don't want to dehydrate them or cause us to have a harder time within the Sundance.

We came out of the Sweat Lodge and shook hands with the others, people I never met in my life, who I knew nothing about. Coming out of the Sweat Lodge is like being born again, by going in there and leaving all our aches, pains and problems. It feels like starting our life all over, without any human or spiritual problems.

In essence, we are all coming from our mother earth's womb, the Sweat Lodge. Some believe that because we sweat together, we become brothers and sisters, although there were no women in the Sweat Lodge with us. We have a separate Sweat Lodge for the women. There were many female Sundancers.

After reaching camp, I had groped around trying to find things. I was sure I knew where everything was. Now I couldn't seem to find anything. It was as though my things had been up walking around that night. It was still dark. Piece by piece I found all the things I needed.

We got ready and then headed back to the Arbor. We took our blankets. They allowed us to take one blanket each and put them under the Arbor. Between songs we could rest and pray. Well, the whole time I am going through this, it sounds like not much is going on, but I was nervous and scared. Understandably enough, I had seen some others get their chest pierced.

I prayed. I asked Grandfather to please help me, to give me the courage to do it well, like a warrior, like a man. Like a person who believes, truly believes, in our spirituality.

I prayed. I saw many other people who were doing the same. I know now there were quite a few new people, just like myself, going in for their first time, although I was one of the older ones.

Then we started lining up. We lined up on the west side of the Arbor. It was nice and cool. I thought, "I should have kept my blanket with me." We couldn't, so we stood there, waiting. I had goosebumps all over my body. There was a beautiful, quiet hush. I could hear the murmur of the people who were still around the fire pit and other Sundancer's voices as they talked quietly. There was no laughing in line. This is a serious thing.

Then from way over on the other side of the Arbor we heard one man hit the drum. It seemed to startle everyone, though we had been waiting for it. It took my breath away. Everything stopped, even the murmurs. Now we were all waiting for the first Eagle whistle to be blown. The drum sounded again.

That sacred drum. The heartbeat of our people sounded to call all the Sundancers, to let them know

it was time to come and get into line. It was time to
see the sun, greet it, and welcome it into our
Sundance, time to sacrifice ourselves for others.

The Sundance Chief blew his Eagle whistle
loudly, three or four times. He started moving
forward. When they saw him move, the drummers
started singing. The slow, and measured beat of the
drum escorted us into the Sundance Arbor.

Then the songs started. Oh, what a beautiful
song it was. I had never heard this song in my life
until now. It gave me goose bumps all up and down
my body. I was choked with pride. I was humbled by
the knowledge that I was listening to the same songs
that Crazy Horse, Sitting Bull and all the other
Sundancers before me had heard. The same songs
they had listened to, I was listening to now.

I was grateful and I felt honored to be in the line
up with the Lakota warriors and warriors from other
different tribes. We started blowing on our Eagle
whistles, first one then another. We kept blowing on
them continuously. The line started moving forward.
I felt the lurch in my stomach again. The time was
drawing near. We were moving forward. I was
starting my first Lakota Sundance. Overwhelmed, I
started blowing my Eagle whistle to keep my
emotions in check.

People from all the different camps had come out
to watch us. They came to see their loved ones,
brothers, cousins, and uncles, going into the
Sundance. To pray and support them.

I prayed, "Grandfather, give me strength and
courage to do this with honor.

They were drumming and singing the "*Going In*"
song. We stopped to honor the four directions, four
times, then we entered the Arbor. When I entered, I
became emotional, yet happy. I was finally at the
Sundance that I had had a vision about so many years

before. I got choked up. I got tears in my eyes. It may not be manly to do this, but I didn't feel bad because I felt I was in the presence of the Creator.

I didn't come there for my ego. I came there, humbled, and I wanted my prayers answered. I wanted my family taken care of. As we went in, we made a complete circle inside the Arbor. Then they went into another song. The beat picked up, making everyone feel good. It was so good to be alive and in the Arbor. By now it was much lighter.

Looking around the Arbor, I was overwhelmed at the sight of so many dancers. Men and women, all beautifully dressed, all there together to pray. There were about 100 of us in there. All the colors the Sundancers wore were bright and beautiful. All the traditional Sundance colors, Red, Yellow, White, Black for the four directions were visible. Also included were Blue for the Sky above, Green for the Earth below and Purple for the Inner Spirit.

We danced and danced. I was finally getting over being cold, dancing was warming up my body. I carried my own sacred, ceremonial pipe on my left arm, as was everyone else. I carried my Eagle wing fan in my right hand. As we danced around the Arbor, I felt great and very proud. I had come so far, and I was finally here.

As the day progressed, we went through all the ceremonies. We greeted the sun, each placed his pipe or "Chanupa" down on the altar. We finished the "Pipe" song, and rested under the arbor. We had been dancing about an hour and a half. Right away I saw other people getting marks on their chest and backs, then they would go out to the tree to release their ropes. This is part of the preparation for their piercing ceremony. My stomach lurched as I watched them, knowing I would be one of them soon. I knew my time for piercing was entirely up to me. It would be done when I asked for it.

That was another thing that made my stomach lurch, how long would it take me to decide? Would I have the courage to walk up to a Sundance leader and say I am ready to pierce? Just the thought made me dizzy and swallow hard. As the realization hit me, that I was here to go through it, I felt alone. My family was not there. Steve and the others were only acquaintances so far. There wasn't a close friend or family member there with me. I had come alone, and I had to stand alone.

There were a couple of Sundancers inside the Arbor who had pierced the day before. I found out that these Sundancers were to stay pierced three or four days. They don't break loose until the last day. It impressed me, their capability of suffering. Their ability to cope with the pain and to withstand all that tugging and pulling on their flesh for four days. It also humbled me. We rested a few minutes, got our blankets situated, and introduced ourselves.

Then, one Sundance leader stood up, and said, "*Ho-ka-hey*, come on, let's go, it's time to dance."

Everybody got up, and being the new one, I followed what everybody else did. I was fortunate to have a few friends to explain a thing or two to me before they happened. We formed the circle and they started singing another song. At the time, I didn't know it was a piercing song. We danced and danced, when I noticed a Sundance leader dancing toward another Sundancer, his feet in perfect rhythm with the beat of the drum. The rhythm of his body movements as he danced and moved around portrayed his confidence and pride. His hair, long and flowing gave him a regal, almost saintly look.

When he reached a Sundancer who was piercing, he was waiting for him. The Sundance leader grabbed his wrist bracelet, and they moved out dancing around the Arbor, then to the Sacred Tree.

You can't believe or understand how I felt inside. The dread that was in me was immense.

I thought, "What am I doing here, why did I make this commitment?" With my next breath, I assured myself, "it's okay, this is your vision, you must be here."

So I started praying, "Grandfather, when I go to pierce, please, give me the energy and the courage to finish. To do it like a man, a warrior, a spiritual person. Please don't allow me to do anything to dishonor my people and the other Sundancers."

It wasn't something I was taking lightly. My stomach was churning, I felt sick. I kept on, and danced hard. I prayed hard. Maybe I was being a little selfish, some of my prayers were for myself. To have the courage to do it right. It's a very hard decision to make, to go there willingly to get pierced. You do it without any anaesthesia or any of the modern conveniences to take away the pain. Just to let somebody else cut your flesh takes trust, and faith in the Creator. I couldn't get it through my head how I was even considering it, but, I was.

I considered it. I thought about it, and I had no choice. I had already made a commitment to do whatever it took. I spoke to other Sundancers.

They told me, "It's a commitment between you and Grandfather. You don't have to do it."

There it was, I had a way out. They told me I didn't have to pierce if I didn't want to. As is human nature, I welcomed a way out, or a way to justify not going through with it. For a few minutes, I thought about not piercing.

Then I thought, "Hey, I'm not looking for a way out. I didn't come all this way from Oklahoma just to back out now."

Fear is little to overcome when the rewards are

so huge. Making that contact with the Creator, having your prayers answered, means so much more than just a little bit of fear or pain. I realized that it was a test by the spirits, when they told me I didn't have to pierce. They had been testing my sincerity and my decision to be there.

We had more Pipe songs, when no one pierced. Then we had more Piercing songs when sometimes as many as six or eight men were pierced.

Many women were dancing and a few were also piercing. They would pierce on their arms or wrists. I'm sure it was just as painful as it was for us. As givers of life, the women brought a very powerful, beautiful and special energy into the Sundance.

Then we would have a piercing song when guys were piercing their backs. They would get tied to several Buffalo skulls, tied together in a row. These skulls would weigh between twenty and thirty pounds each. Depending on the dancer they would tie, three or more skulls together for the dancer to drag.

The reason the buffalo is honored, by dragging the skulls, is to give back all that the buffalo has given to us. He gave his blood, flesh, pain and life for us, so we could have nourishment to survive. He gave us abundance in all ways. This was our way to show respect and gratitude for "*Tatanka*," our buffalo brother, and the sacred tradition. Also we respect the buffalo because we believe that it is the bringer of courage and strength both physical and spiritual.

When all the dancers piercing their chests were through, the ones piercing their backs were next. That made the song very long. I've danced songs that lasted three hours. It was hard, we were very happy to finish that kind of song.

It was really hot. I was still tired from two weeks before when I had Sundanced in Wyoming. Now this was my second Sundance in a matter of two weeks. It takes quite a few days to recuperate when you have gone through a Sundance. I was still not normal from that first one. This Lakota Sundance was quite different from the Shoshoni one, but it was still hard on me.

Here again we had different drum groups that came to sing and drum for us. As has happened on occasion, sometimes we were short on drummers. There would be Pow Wow's going on in the immediate area within a hundred and fifty miles. Many drums go to the Pow Wows instead of coming to Sundances. At the Sundances it's all voluntary, strictly free, they don't ask for any money. They are fed and they're given all they want to drink.

No money changes hands because they are doing it for a spiritual ceremony. So, on occasion we couldn't get enough drums. We would have one or two drum groups to sing, and it made it hard on them. So, they had to rest quite a bit. Since all liquids, water and foods are forbidden around the Arbor, they had to stop and go to camp or somebody else's camp to eat. So, we rested until they came back, without drummers and singers we can't dance.

This time we had it pretty good. We had three different drum groups. They kept us busy dancing. We danced and finished out the day. They allowed us to return to camp, and it's on an honor system. Nobody holds an axe over your head and says you can't do this, or that. You made the commitment with the Creator, nobody watches you. If anyone does anything wrong, they answer the Creator.

This is one of things I learned. In the Sundance don't try to be judgmental of everything and everyone. Let people do their own thing, as you do yours. Each of us has a mind of our own and what is right for one person is wrong for another. That doesn't mean that it is wrong for both. It only means that we think differently. We should try to honor and respect other people's way of thinking.

Anyways, as that day ended, I felt good. I felt energized and that the spirits had been with me. My guides had led me to the right place. If I felt that I had fallen in love with the first Sundance that was with the Shoshoni people, I felt even more so with the Lakota people. I felt I was home.

The other things I had gone through were almost like stepping stones to get me to where I was now.

I woke up early the next morning, because of the anticipation of the day ahead. I've never been one to need a clock or anything like that. At 3:45 am, I was awake. By 4:30 they started calling us.

"Sundancers, come on down. This is not the Holiday Inn, get up its time to go! The sweats are ready. Its time to get up, Sundancers!"

So, I got up. Steve was already up. He said, "I'm up. Let's get going, Manny."

As we headed for the Sweat Lodges, I knew something was different about my energy. I felt light headed. I believe I was also feeling the Sundance energy. It's a very tangible thing when you're willing to receive it. For the first time, since taking the Sundance path, I felt strangely at peace with myself and completely unafraid. It wasn't resignation, it was a calm acceptance of whatever the Creator was bringing me. I felt so light on my feet, as if I were gliding, instead of walking to the Sweat Lodges. For a moment I thought maybe my blood pressure was high, but everything was wonderful.

Since developing high blood pressure, sometimes in the Sweat Lodge, I find it difficult to breathe and my blood pressure goes up. Incidentally, I'm not even supposed to go into Sweat Lodges, according to my doctor, but, I do it anyways. It's difficult sometimes to catch my breath. I don't know if it's a residue from smoking. I walked up to the fire pit area where they had the fires going to keep the rocks hot. I saw this other man there. His name is Keith.

Keith looked at me and said, "Come on." He waved at me with his hand. "Join me in the sweat."

I went in right behind him. The Sweat Lodge filled quickly. There were about thirteen men in there. They brought the rocks in. We sprinkled them with cedar, and thanked the Creator for the past two days. Although, I had only been in one of them.

We thanked him for allowing us to Sundance on this third day, and Keith started singing the "*Four Directions*" song in there.

I had never been able to sing in there because the heat was so intense. Being unable to catch my breath, didn't allow me to sing. Suddenly, I found myself clear headed. My throat was so clear, I felt a big bubble of joy just burst inside me. When I started singing, I sang the whole song with Keith.

I said to myself, "Today I pierce. I pierce first round, first song."

Once I made that commitment, I felt elated. Oh, I couldn't believe that I was making a commitment to let someone cut into my chest so my prayers would be heard. The feeling is unexplainable. I felt like crying. I felt very, very humble, as if I were finally there. This is the way the Sundance is.

Each time you learn something more about the Sundance and experience something new, you feel as if you've reached a higher plateau of spiritual understanding. As if you arrived at another place. It's like adding little pebbles, little stones to the entire pile that is you. You add those small stones one at a time. Each of them brings a bit more knowledge.

No matter who we are or how knowledgeable we are, we never stop learning. We never know it all. The Creator is so infinite that he is always feeding little titbits of information and knowledge so we can become better persons. I cherish every little piece of information, every little stone that I can add to that pile. I'm grateful that with all this, the Creator also gives us choices and free will.

Coming out of the Sweat Lodge, I headed back to camp and never said anything to Steve, or anybody. I went through the motions to get ready as though in a dream, everything was close by me. I dressed in three minutes, and was ready. When I got to the Arbor, the first person I saw was Keith.

I said, "Brother." I shook his right hand with both of my hands, "Thank you, thank you very much for a wonderful sweat this morning."

To the puzzled look on his face I explained about my trouble breathing in the Sweat Lodge, because of my high blood pressure.

"Keith, it was the first time I have been able to sing this song all the way through. I feel that it was you, that inspired me to sing the way I did."

"I am happy that you sang it with us. Manny, thank you for showing gratitude and respect like this. Not too many people think about it anymore. Though we are spiritual, we forget to give credit where it's due. Thank you for that."

Then I told him, "When we go in, I'm piercing first round."

"Ho! I'm glad to hear that," he said smiling.

He knew I was a new man. He knew I had only danced yesterday, but my spiritual energy was so high that he also knew it was time for me to pierce.

He asked, "When did you decide, when did you know?"

"When we were singing the four directions song together, I knew it was time for me to go."

He said, "Okay, it'll be done just the way you want it." Then I realized that the "Four Directions" song had taken me back to my vision. To when the Spotted Eagle and I, had soared high in the heavens. When he had shown me where I was to the help people, in the four directions.

Now, mentally and emotionally I was ready. Physically, I hoped I was, I didn't know what my tolerance for pain was. I smashed my fingers and, stubbed my toes a few times. I'd even cut myself accidentally in my life. I'd had tooth aches and headaches, but could I cope with this? Did I have strength, and courage to go through this ceremony? After thanking Keith, I went and sat by myself in the Arbor on my blanket.

I felt so alone. I guess that's the way life is, when a person faces a challenge. He might have support from friends or relatives but ultimately we must face pain, heartbreak or personal trials alone.

I prayed for guidance. I prayed for direction.

All the spirits where coming to me and saying, "This is the time. You are at the right place. It is your turn to offer your flesh, blood, pain and suffering for the people you want healed. Don't worry. You are ready."

With that in mind, I felt elated. I was walking on air, this was my reality that morning. It was a fresh morning in South Dakota. The fire pit, the Sweat Lodge, Grandfather's breath, the steam that comes off the stones, all made memories for me. It stayed burned in my mind, remembering my first piercing Sundance, my first Lakota Sundance.

Now being a bit wiser I was committing myself, to another four years. I did it without any remorse, or hesitation, without expectations, except to ask for blessings from the Creator.

We lined up again. The Sundance Chief started blowing his Eagle whistle, we moved forward. I waited for the dread and fear to start in the pit of my

stomach. My wait was in vain, it never arrived. As
we entered the Arbor from the east side, I felt myself
calmed by the sound of the drums.

We greeted the sun, prayed and danced for over
an hour and a half. It was a beautiful first song. We
placed our pipes "*Chanupa's*," at the altar and went
to our blankets to rest.

Keith walked up to me and asked, "Is this it?"

I looked at him, eye to eye. I replied "This is it
brother."

"Okay where do you want to pierce?"

I pointed to the places on my chest.

He asked, "Once, or twice?"

"Let's go for both sides. I came a long way from
Oklahoma to get pierced on only one side."

He took the time to explain to me, "Manny, this
is your first time, are you sure you want both sides?
Most new guys and first timers, will only pierce once
to make sure they can endure the pain."

"I'm sure, I want both sides done. I can do it.
The spirits came to me this morning and told me that
I was ready."

He says, "That's fine. It's all up to you. You're
the boss." So, he marked both sides of my chest.
When my friends saw that my chest was marked,
they came and shook my hand. They told me to be
strong, to have courage.

One Sundance leader, Lessert, said, "Manny, it's
painful, but you're a warrior. Don't worry."

"Lessert, I want you and Norbert to do the
piercing for me, will you?"

Laughingly he replied, "You bet we will, how
many you want?"

He turned away from me and yelled at the
drummers, "*ho-ka-hey*. It's time to go, lets go
Sundancers. Get ready."

After Keith marked my chest, I asked Steve if I

could use his rope. Steve had gone out with me, we untied the rope and laid it out. By now I had time to think again, my stomach and brain was turning. I was getting very nervous. My heart was beating faster and faster. I kept telling myself, this was my decision. This is where I should be. This is where the Creator wanted me to be.

As I sit here writing this, I feel almost as much apprehension as I did then. It wasn't fear, now that I think about it, maybe it was anxiety because of stepping into the unknown. Although I knew I was going to go through it, I still felt a dread. I just didn't know my tolerance for pain, but I would soon find out. The next song started, and Lessert yelled, "*Ho-ka-hey.*" We all got in line in our appropriate places and danced out. Every time we danced, we ended up in the same spot. I felt good.

From then on it was almost like a whirlwind of action. A man who became a very dear friend of mine from Maryland, Henry. He's a professor of art at the University of Maryland. He knew I was going to pierce because of the marks on my chest. He grabbed my wrist and pushed me out of my spot. This way the Sundance leaders know I was piercing.

Keith danced up to me and said, "You ready?"

I said, "I'm ready." He grabbed my sage wrist bracelet, and took me around the Arbor. Always going clockwise until we got to the west side.

He took me to the tree, and said, "Brother, you are going to experience something very, very sacred. You are going to be very close to God, to the Creator. Make the most of this time because you will be one on one with him right now."

Keith continued, "This tree is a sacred tree. It'll give you confidence and courage. It's representative of God. Ask it for whatever you want. Give it your prayers, respect, your honor, and it will do as you wish. This is the place where many good men, good warriors come to pray."

Then he left me, and I stood there for a few minutes. I prayed, I felt a reluctance to leaving the tree, when a Sundance Leader came and asked me, "Are you ready?"

It seemed everything started to move in slow motion. I often wondered why, when something dramatic is going to happen, we say things were slower. The only reason I can think of, is when a person anticipates something happening, suddenly its not happening fast enough.

I replied with a nervous smile, "I am ready."

They laid me down on a buffalo robe. That's where they lay people down to pierce them.

I handed them my scalpel.

They took the crown off my head.

They said to put it in my mouth.

They told me to bite down on my crown, because it is very painful.

Lessert said, "If you will pray, and pray hard to the Creator it won't hurt because he'll be answering your prayers."

I lay there on my back, on the ground looking into the sky. Then handed him my piercing bones. He got on his knees next to me, and his father knelt on my left side.

I felt both of them grab my chest and rub it with some dirt, because I was sweaty and slippery. This way their thumb and finger won't slip.

They pinched up my skin and I felt as the knife went into my flesh.

I felt a sharp, sharp intense pain in my chest.

As if somebody had put a red hot iron on my flesh.

I lost all sense of time.

I couldn't hear any sounds.

I didn't feel the heat of the sun.

I tried to grit my teeth. I couldn't, my crown was in my mouth.

I prayed to the Creator to give me strength, to give me courage. I was doing it for my children.

Then I felt them do something else.

They were putting my piercing bone through the wound.

As he was tying it up, I felt something my left side of my chest. I was concentrating so much on my prayers, to me it felt like somebody tugging on my arm, I really didn't notice. When Les got through tying my rope around my piercing bone, he and his father grabbed my arms.

Les said, "Come on, get up. You're done."

I said, "Wait a minute, Lessert. I want both sides pierced."

He said, "They are."

I looked down, and you know what, I was pierced on the left side too. Yet, I felt absolutely nothing. I felt nothing because my prayers to the Creator gave me courage and strength to endure.

When standing up, I did feel pain. I felt pain, but I also felt that closeness with the Creator. I felt like crying for all the people who needed my prayers. I prayed they could get enough to eat. I prayed for all the people who are sick in the world. It brought tears to my eyes. It shamed me to have tears appear, because I thought if the other dancers see them they might think I am crying because of the pain. The pain did not compare to what I was receiving from this sacred experience.

Lessert told me to go ahead and get into place, wherever I wanted to dance. I pulled my rope, and danced out. I was dancing because they were still drumming and singing. It was still going on. I will never forget those songs. They are so beautiful, so calming. I went out as far as my rope would reach. I leaned back and the flesh on my chest pulled out tight. As I was praying to the tree, I could feel the pain in my chest. All my friends had come around to stand behind me, and give me support, to receive that energy from me. All that energy I was going to pull down from the sun to help us, to help answer our prayers.

Through my mind were thoughts of disbelief I was actually doing this. Every time I leaned back on my rope, I felt intense pain in my chest. It became a raw ache that reached all the way down to my toes. Every time I looked at my piercing bones, I saw the faces of my children. I knew this was for their protection and my way of giving my pain for them. Scary, yes . . . Painful, yes . . . Rewarding, you bet. This was why Grandfather brought me here.

All my friends were there. Steve, Larry, Keith, Lessert and many others, they had all come over. Although he had to support all the other dancers, Lessert and people I barely knew, were there to stand by me. Without my family, I was really there alone. Steve's sister, Chrys, and other friends that had come with them, stood by me.

It felt glorious, beautiful, and explosive. The energy was high and brilliant. I danced and then Lessert waved at me with his fan.

He said, "Ho-ka!" He meant as he pointed at the tree, "Go to the tree and pray."

I got to the tree and knelt beside it and put my arms around it. I thought of my mother and father. I asked, "*Tunkashila*" Grandfather, to watch over them, then danced back to my spot and pulled back on the rope again.

One dancer next to me, whispered, "Pull back, pull it tight. Stretch your flesh. It will break easier when you're ready to break loose."

Looking into my eyes, Steve danced in front of me with his Eagle fan, he started tapping and hitting on my rope in a downward motion. He was trying to help me stretch the flesh.

I smiled at him and said, "*Wo-Pila*," "thank you, Steve."

Again, Les waved his Eagle fan and yelled, "Ho-ka-hey."

Then I went back to the tree and prayed the second time. Embracing the tree, I could smell the warm cloth wrapped around it. It felt soft, because of so much cloth. Many people tied all this cloth on the tree, as prayer ties. They wanted their prayers answered. I danced back to my spot.

Then he yelled, "Ho-ka," the third time.

I went to the tree and prayed. I prayed for everyone that I could think of. I prayed for people I didn't know, I prayed for all those who I may meet during the coming year. There is so much to pray about. So many people that need prayers, it boggles the mind to remember people by name, or try to remember those who need your prayers to heal them.

Finally he said, "Ho-ka," for the fourth and last time.

I danced back to the sacred tree. Again, I embraced it. I knew that when I left here I would be breaking free from it. It would be like separating myself from my mother. Breaking the umbilical cord that attached me to her. I would be free. I prayed for the courage to break loose on my first attempt.

Lessert walked up to me and said, "When you go this time, go fast, go hard. You have to break loose, it is the only way you can get off this rope, is to break away and tear the flesh out. So run backwards fast, don't worry, those guys will catch you."

I prayed to Grandfather.

"This is it. You brought me this far, please don't

fail me now. Give me the courage to finish this piercing ceremony like a man, like a warrior."

As I finished my prayer, I started running back.

I went back, back. I looked at the tree and said silently, "Grandfather, please give me strength."

I am going faster, and faster, and faster.

I hit the end of the line.

I heard my flesh tear, rip and pop.

I saw the rope bouncing way up into the tree.

It dangled there for a second, then dropped.

While this was going on, I fell backwards.

I had broken loose.

It's really surprising how strong the flesh is. It doesn't tear that easy. It took all my strength and weight to break loose. Steve, and a couple of the other Sundancers caught me when I fell.

I was so happy, I let out a big yell. I jumped up and down. I had finally done what I envisioned at that Shoshoni Sundance, so long ago. I was at the top of my spiritual being then. My energy was flashing. The energy around me was sparking many people. They gained a lot, I feel, because my energy was so hot. I brought that sun power down on myself and all the people who came to support me.

Steve grabbed my arm bracelet, and took me around the Arbor to my spot. As I ran by the other Sundancers they were all patting me on the shoulder.

Most of them were men who had pierced in the past who knew about the pain, the happiness, the jubilation. All or most would pierce before the weekend was over. That's another commitment that is only between you and the Creator. Nobody has to pierce. Only the ones who make the commitment with the Creator have to go through that ceremony.

Steve left me back in my spot where I had started. I felt high, like I had reached that ultimate plateau of human spirituality. I found out that I was wrong, there was more to follow.

After several Sundances, I realized that this was not the ultimate. There are other plateaus to experience. New heights of awareness to achieve in the Sundance circle, and other circles as well. This was just the beginning of my journey.

We finished that Saturday evening. After getting out, I walked around visiting other people, other camps, wearing my scars like badges of honor, that I was proud to have. Although it isn't seen as showing off, it's viewed as an honorable thing we have done. The piercing of the flesh, the giving of our pain, blood and flesh so others may live well.

There are similarities between the Lakota Sundance and the Shoshoni Sundance. The main difference is piercing. The principle is the same. You never go in there to pray for yourself, always to pray for others.

I went in because I had so many people that needed prayers, my parents, my sisters and brother. It appears the Creator chose me, from my family, to be the Sundancer. I feel honored. This is why I felt that I had to be there.

Saturday evening, I thanked Norbert Running, the Sundance Chief, I said I would like to stay, but I have to get back to Oklahoma. It's going to take all day Sunday to get back. I said I have left my family unattended without money and have to go.

He said, "You came, you danced, you pierced, you have to go, everybody understands including the Creator. The commitment you made was to him and not to me."

I begged off and early next morning left for Oklahoma. I got there as predicted Sunday evening. My wife was a little upset because I pierced. I knew it bothered her, but she didn't make it a big issue.

Later when I went to California, I met some

Sundancers, during that winter. I was spending quite a bit of time in California selling.

I left Oklahoma in January to do a show in Santa Monica. I stayed out there because we needed the money.

Around this time, I finished a movie script. That was the best place to try to sell it and would mean a great deal of money for my family.

I stayed out in California after that big show.

My wife was making crafts at home, while I made them in California. With the crafts that she sent me, I was doing really well and always sending money home.

A couple of times I thought about going home, but my wife kept talking me out of it. She reminded me that the best place to sell the script was in California.

It was hard for me, I missed my family, it was almost three months now since I had left.

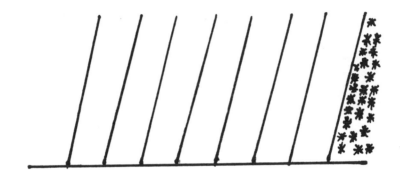

NORTH - RED

"Cold Winds"
Snow

Well, by the middle of that May, I guess my wife decided she had enough of that kind of life.

Once I was talking to her, chatting about what was going on. Our conversation was a little tense, but nothing special I thought. She wanted us to invest in a trailer, and I said no. So she said, "I guess that's all I have to say, I'll talk to you later. I love you."

I didn't answer her, I just hung up.

The next morning, I received an overnight letter from my wife. She told me not to bother coming back, she didn't want to hurt me anymore. I didn't understand that statement then. I do now.

It seems I went into a state of shock. I couldn't believe what I was reading. After fifteen years of marriage, I never expected to hear this. Other than our talk the day before, everything seemed fine.

What hurt the most was the thought of being left out of my children's lives. She would have had to write the letter about the time she was talking to me, but she hadn't let on she felt this way.

She wrote, "This life is over, I am tired of being a telephone wife."

I couldn't blame her. I understood. By this time, I got to where I didn't even miss her or my kids as much as before. That frightened me. It was like they almost ceased to mean anything to me.

I started praying to Grandfather.

I said, "Grandfather, what's happening to me. I'd hoped for a better life, this is why I Sundanced."

The realization hit me that this was really happening. It hit me hard, I blamed myself, then I became consumed with anger toward my wife. Then I blamed myself some more. My mental state started to deteriorate. Filled with grief, remorse, even bitterness, I felt abandoned.

In my attempts to pray, I felt even Grandfather had left me behind. When you're beating yourself up, you don't think you're worthy of Grandfather's help. Then I rationalized in my head for awhile, that this may be a good thing. Maybe I was supposed to be free again. Well, when this happened, I started drinking. I drank to dull the pain.

When I ran out of booze, I would feel the pain over the loss of my children. Deeply hurt, I drank for about a month. I felt a rage against this woman that had done this to me. I had trusted her completely. I had never questioned anything she did. Yet, suddenly, she told me not to come home.

All this time, I was wandering aimlessly. From place to place, from pow wow to pow wow. Once at a Pow Wow in Cupertino, I was dancing competition in the arena. My mind wasn't on dancing, because of my emotional state. The song was a *"Sneak Up,"* a special dance for hunters or warriors.

I didn't realize I was dancing the wrong way for that song, until one dancer casually danced near and informed me it was a "Sneak Up." Embarrassed, I just turned and walked out of the arena.

Tom, the MC and friend, made an excuse for me. He said, "Sometimes us old timers go to so many pow wows that we forget one song from the other." He knew what I was going through. Everyone did, and they tried to help me through it.

I went outside and looked off in the distance. I didn't know that someone was taking a picture of me. It's the one on the cover of this book. The woman who took it had to try to capture the moment. She told me about it later and asked my permission. She promised to send me a copy, which she did.

Now looking at the picture, it seems to say everything. Right then, my mind was on my loss.

The Creator had decided to take away all that I held dear to me, my family.

The feeling of grief and devastation was hard to take, and I realized then that all I had now was the Sundance. The Creator was teaching me to depend on my spirituality for strength. The pain would pass in time, but the Sundance or my spiritual foundation would be forever.

After that I was still wondering what I had done. Why did this happen? I blamed myself for the whole entire month while I was drinking.

Then suddenly, one morning I woke up. I was in Monterey, at a campground. I rolled over, sat up in bed and grabbed a bottle of beer. I took a drink.

Then I stopped and I looked at the bottle, then at the mess I called a bed. I looked at the over flowing bag of dirty clothes. I looked at myself and what I had become in one month. I didn't like what I saw.

Then I asked myself, "What in the world are you doing? You are having a beer for breakfast. This is absurd. You've never had a drink this early in your life, why now?"

I checked my pockets and only found three dollars left. Then I checked the crafts box. It was empty. Well here I was, almost flat broke, no food, no crafts and no prospects. Again I thought to myself, my God, what am I doing to myself?

I got up, took a shower and shaved. I felt better than I had in days. I headed out and stopped at a big hardware and craft store.

I walked around, debating whether to do what I had in mind. It bothered me to consider stealing what I needed, to make some money. Ironically, the items I needed, were to make one of our spiritual symbols, the medicine wheel.

I took a deep breath, and decided that above all I had to survive. This is the only way that I knew how. I asked forgiveness.

Then I went and found the largest shammy cloth that they had. It was smooth, soft and pliable leather. I walked around the store so long until finally, I slipped it into my shirt. I paid for the other couple of items that were under a dollar, and I walked out.

I don't do this kind of thing. I got scared, scared that I might be stopped. That I could be caught and thrown in jail for that little piece of shammy cloth, but I needed that leather to make those medicine wheels. I needed something to sell, to make, to buy myself some food and some gas, at least to get myself going again.

I was down at the bottom.

I was scraping bottom.

I didn't know what I was going to do. I didn't even have enough money left to pay for another night at the campground. So here I am, feeling forced, or maybe I'd forced myself into this nasty situation. I stopped my van in a parking lot. It wasn't too far from where I had taken, or should I say, stolen that piece of shammy cloth.

I cut up the leather into strips. I wrapped the wooden hoops I used to make medicine wheels. The spirits were with me, the Creator was also close to me in my time of need.

Everything went so smoothly, so fast, and they turned out beautiful. I finished them in record time. I knew of this little store, in Pacific Grove. So I went there.

I went in, and showed her what I had. The girl said, "Oh my God, you've got medicine wheels? I have had more calls for these in the last couple of weeks, I'll take all six of them. I'll need more, how many can you make me."

I said, "As many as you want."

She said, "Make me another thirty, then I'll have

thirty-six. Then I'll have three dozen and that'll hold me for a good part of the summer."

I asked, "Would it be possible to get a little advance on the order? I need to buy leather and stuff to make them with."

She said, "Sure, I'll give you half the cost of my order. Okay?"

I figured, she had bought the six, paid for that and the deposit on the other thirty put me in good shape. Good, I was happy, now things were starting to look much better.

I went and had a good breakfast. I returned to the same store where I had taken the leather. I was afraid to go to the manager and admit what I had done because I felt terrible. I felt so guilty, I thought that maybe they could still throw me in jail. I was ashamed to admit it.

Instead of doing that, I went in there and I bought all the supplies I needed. I wanted to compensate or say sorry for what I'd done. I bought more than enough to make the other thirty medicine wheels. I felt a little better about it, but it has always sat badly with me and I've never forgotten it.

I've tried to drum up the courage a couple of times to stop in and say, "Hey, back in so and so year, I took this." But I've been too ashamed to admit it.

I have been into that store on two other occasions since then. I've always bought more things than I need. That piece of shammy has cost me quite a bit because of my guilty feelings.

I feel that the Creator forgave me because my life has returned to normal. I never blamed anyone for my actions and the situation I found myself in.

I finished her order and that gave me plenty of money. I went back and I got gas in my van. I bought more supplies and went right back up to that same campground. I made some shields, I made this, I made that. I bought leather, beads, feathers, everything that I needed and within a couple of weeks I was back on my feet. I was forgetting the pain or at least it had diminished. I was feeling a lot better about myself. I could take the heartache a little bit better.

So I headed back down toward Los Angeles. I drove on to Torrance and went to see my native brother, Wolfhawk. We went out to dinner. While we were eating, the subject got around to the recent changes in my life.

I said, "Wolfhawk, I don't know what I did wrong. I don't know where I messed up, where I screwed up."

He said, "Manny, let me tell you something. I've seen you work and work many hours. Putting the welfare of your family first, above your own comforts. I've watched you send money, and more money home."

He continued, "You didn't screw up, she did. It's not you're fault, man. I wondered how long it would take you to realize it. Apparently you haven't let yourself see it yet. So it's my job to tell you, to let you know, that it was not you who screwed up. It was her."

He said, "Let it go. Send money to the kids. Tell them that you love them every chance you get. Write to them on their birthdays, on Christmas, on Easter. Send them a card, send them $20, $30, a $100 dollars, when you can. Remember always to tell them that you love them so they won't forget you."

I took his advice and I started doing it. It wasn't long after that, I saw some friends of mine up in San Juan Baptista. They were going to their first Sundance, there was four of them.

I told them, "Look guys, it's pretty tough there

and I'm an old hand at it now. I've been to one
Lakota Sundance and I had four under my belt at the
other place, so I'm an old timer to the Sundance
circle. I'll be there the day before, to support you
when you go in the Arbor. I'll be there Wednesday
night to help you. I'll give you any advice and help
that I can."

Meanwhile, I was learning how to make this
new/old article called the "Dream Catcher." Many
people are familiar with it. It was becoming very
popular.

It all started when I decided to teach myself how
to make them. When I made the first one, several of
my friends saw it and laughed.

They said, "That one is for nightmares, not for
dreams."

I thought it was pretty good, but I wasn't quite
getting the stitch right. I racked my brain trying to
figure it out.

I was at this little Pow-Wow in Fresno,
California and I ran into this good friend of mine
from Bakersfield. She is a wonderful little lady. Her
name is *Wia Chanupa*, meaning "Pipe Woman." She
took one look at my dream catcher and said, "God,
Manny, that looks awful. I wouldn't show that to
anybody! Well, you've almost got it. The only thing
you're missing is this."

She showed me once, and I said, "Oh man,
that's so simple, I can't believe it."

"Another day and you'd have figured it out
yourself."

When she showed me that simple step, I got
busy making more dream catchers.

I never did fix that first one I made, but
apparently it didn't matter. I was at a Pow-Wow one
time and this girl from across the arena saw it and
came running.

She said, "I'll take that dream catcher."

"Well, it's $60.00."

"It's okay, I'll take it."

After paying me, she said, "if it was $150.00, I would still have bought it."

I said, "Well you know, I want you to be happy."

"Oh, no, that's okay. Sixty is fine."

By this time, I was doing all right with them.

At times, I would sit in my van, right on the beach for a week, and make dream catchers. It was very hard to sit there alone hour after hour, working. It gave me time to think. I felt sometimes like my chest was going to burst, I missed my kids so much.

When the thinking became too painful, I would get out of the van and ride my bike up and down the Strand at Redondo Beach. Just to be around other people until I was too tired to think any more.

Back then, I knew of three or four other people who were making dream catchers commercially. All of us were doing really, really well.

Dream Catchers are old. Traditionally, the Sioux and the Ojibwa used them for spiritual and emotional healing.

Long ago, they were only made by the medicine man in the tribe. He would be called on if someone was having difficulty sleeping, or having nightmares. The medicine man would consult the spirits, then make a dream catcher for that individual.

He went through many prayers and a sacred ceremony while making each dream catcher. They considered it bad medicine for anyone else to create one for any other reason or any other way.

I headed up to South Dakota and got there the day they were going in to the Sundance. I pulled in about seven o'clock in the evening. The boys were sitting in the teepee. They were really happy to see me. They were as anxious and frightened as I had been my first time. Don't misunderstand me, you never really get used to it.

I sat and talked with them way past midnight finally, it was time to go to sleep. I left them alone and went to bed.

In the morning when they went in, I encouraged and wished them luck. They all danced and pierced that first day.

It was important to me to be there when they went in because I had been alone for my first piercing Sundance. I was glad they had each other for company. I felt that I had done my job by keeping my word to them that I would be there. I was proud, proud of all of them.

There were four Sundance brothers, Jessie, Sonny, Lonnie and Marty. Shortly after the piercing ceremony, I said goodbye and left.

Marty did not pierce that first year because he had not made that commitment to Grandfather. Personally I think if he never pierces it's good. He is a Vietnam Veteran (173rd Airborne) and badly wounded in action. I feel he has given enough pain, flesh and blood for all of us. He is a good warrior and nephew!

I had another brother, Lionel, who was going into his first Sundance over in Porcupine, South Dakota. I had told him I would help him prepare for his "*Hanblecheya*" vision quest and his Sundance.

When I got there Lionel was kneeling down doing something. He looked over toward me and said to himself, "That van sure looks like Manny's van." Then he looked closer at me and said, "by gosh, it looks like Manny too!" He finally got a good look at me and standing up, smiling he said, "I just can't believe it, it is you Manny! You did come to help me."

The weather was really hot and muggy. I stopped the van and got out. Smiling, I said, "hey brother, how's it going?"

We shook hands and hugged, he motioned for me to sit and asked if I wanted something to drink. He had his tent pitched right under a very nice, shady tree. He had been there a few days already, getting the Arbor prepared for the Sundance.

I noticed that he was a little nervous and apprehensive. This was his first time to dance and pierce. He was really happy to see me. A familiar, friendly face from home.

I mention fear or being afraid, yet, I have never mentioned anyone backing out, or backing down from that challenge or commitment. It's a funny thing, once you have made that commitment to the Creator, you won't allow yourself to back out. Even if you want to.

It is such a sacred and special act. It goes so deep into you that you don't even consider backing out.

Anyways, we spent the afternoon visiting, drinking coffee and talked about mutual friends. I told him about Sonny, Jessie, Lonnie and Marty. They were also friends of his. It comforted him to know his friends had just gone through their first piercing ceremony.

Later that evening, I volunteered to go to Rapid City, to buy whatever we needed.

After eating, I helped him put his crown together, his ankle and his wrist bracelets. We made some tobacco ties to put on the Sacred Tree. I helped him gets his flags ready and the little altar for his "*Chanupa*," his pipe.

We had coffee late that night. By this time all our major visiting was done. We sat there for long moments in silence, feeding small sticks into the campfire. From time to time, others would stop and visit, then leave. It was so pleasant, to sit and relax, after so much driving. That cup of coffee was a good way to end the day.

This was also the time when I got to meet a great man, the Sundance Chief.

I had met a gentle man.

His energy was quiet, and unassuming, yet so powerful. He has got the energy that others are seeking. He comes by his spirituality quite naturally, from a people whose very existence depends on their deep spiritual beliefs. I deeply respect this man, and he's the man I follow in the Sundance.

His name is David Swallow, Jr. He runs the Sundance up at Porcupine, South Dakota. When I got there, as I was driving in, I spotted a good, secluded area.

This is where the Sundance Arbor is. They mow and rake the area around there every year to make it into a decent campground for people who come to the Sundance. There's no electricity, or running water. The only conveniences are what you bring with you.

The only place to get water is at David's old ranch house. It has to be the best water well in the country. It's very deep, and very cold water. You get the water by using the old-fashioned pump that's over the well. Every time I drink it, I think it should be bottled and distributed all over. It would sure benefit David and his family a lot.

Anyways, getting back to David. Following tradition, I went to him and took him some tobacco. I told him what had happened to me with my family, how I was hurting and missing my kids. I had found him sitting behind Lionel's tent drinking a cup of coffee and talking with Al and Bernice. When he knew that what I had to discuss was important to me, he stood up. We started walking away from the others.

He told me some things. What he said made me realize there may be a good reason this happened. I won't get into the details. I respected what he had told me and I accepted it.

He said, "The only thing you can do now is pray for your children. Pray that maybe some day they will return to you."

"When they grow up, they will want their dad. They'll want to know where you are. They'll want to be with you."

He said, "Meanwhile, pray for them, and pray hard. The biggest thing is pray for forgiveness for your wife."

He continued, "I don't believe it was her fault. Circumstances pushed you two apart, and maybe through prayer she'll reconsider."

"No," I replied, "I have too much pride. It is over."

There was a long pause. We had both stopped walking. He stood for a long quiet moment, I stood waiting. Finally as if he had received confirmation from the spirits, he nodded his head.

As we started walking back to camp, he said, "Well if it is over, just be strong, and take the best road open to you, the Sundance."

David asked me, "Did you come to dance?"

"I came to visit and help support Lionel."

"*Washtelo*, good," he answered, "Please make yourself at home. You're always welcome here."

After our talk we returned to camp for more coffee.

When we got there, there were three other young men that impressed me. Bo was one of David Swallow's Sundance Leaders. He was also the Women Sundance Leader, Pansy's son. Marvin and

Tony had married Al and Bernice's two daughters. They were Sundancers, Drummers and Singers, and respectful young men.

I spent seven wonderful days there. I went to Rapid City, returned with the things we needed, and some things we didn't. The days passed, sometimes slow, sometimes fast, but always hot. Every evening was a blessed relief, it always cooled off.

David took Lionel up to the mountain on his vision quest.

Before he left, I said, "Brother, if you need anything, spiritually, please let me know. I'll be in tune with your energy. Send a message if you need help, and I'll be with you."

I was fast asleep. About 1:30, 2:00, in the morning I felt something hit the side of my van. It startled me, and I woke up instantly. Then there was another louder thump, further away from me toward the front. The first one had been right at my side door where I sleep. The next time it moved further forward, and then right up at the front there were three small bangs on the front bumper. It worked its way around to the driver's side, and when it got even with me, it stopped. I jumped up and looked around.

I thought maybe someone I just met was trying to scare me or pull a joke on me. I looked and no one was there. It was dark, but I could see well enough. There are no lights except moon and star light. It was very brilliant. I couldn't spot anybody.

It got me thinking, "What is this?" Then I swallowed hard and realized, "My God, my brother Lionel is in trouble. He's asking for my help."

So, I got up found my smudging shell and grabbed a big piece of medicine sage. After finding my lighter, I lit the sage.

I got out of my van and started praying. "Grandfather, please help those three."

There had been three to go up. I was asking help
for all three of them. It could possibly be one of the
others asking for help. I forget exactly what I was
saying, but I know I was praying hard for them to
have the courage and strength to do their
"*Hanblecheya.*"

"Help those warriors make it through the night.
Help them find their direction and advice," I asked
Grandfather. I knew that one of them was in trouble
and I thought it was my brother Lionel.

Suddenly, off in the distance I heard David start
drumming and singing. Apparently he also knew that
someone needed help. His voice and the drum were
hauntingly beautiful. Muted by distance, the sound
seemed to come from out of the past.

Two days later when they came down from their
vision quest, it was revealed who it was.

I was sitting, drinking a cup of coffee. I had just
finished eating. David was leaving to go get them
from their vision quest, they had been up there for
two days and two nights. Besides Lionel, there was
two others that went up, one was a white boy from
Nebraska, the other was Lakota from Pineridge.

The Lakota boy was the one who had the
problems. He got scared and was hallucinating. He
thought everybody had forgotten about him. He
walked back down.

If a person walks away from the "*Hanblecheya*"
sight, by himself, he has committed a terrible
sacrilege. When he is seeking a vision and leaves
without the spiritual people that took him up there,
they consider it bad medicine for him and his family.
It is disrespectful of the Great Spirit and of that
ceremony. Bad things can happen.

Not only that, it is very embarrassing for the
relatives or anyone associated with this young man.
Anyways, he came down when he shouldn't have. He

talked to me and the others. I didn't realize it at the time, but even I wasn't supposed to acknowledge his presence. Acknowledging him breaks the spiritual energy from the "*Hanblecheya.*"

He asked me where everybody was, and I told him that David had gone up to get him. Embarrassed he was nervously trying to explain why he had come down. I am not going into it because it is an embarrassment to him, and very personal.

The experience humbled me. Many people would judge him harshly. "*Hanblecheya*" is a hard thing to do. Anyone who would judge a person like that should first walk in their moccasins. I think it made me realize how serious all this is. It's very sacred, the "*Hanblecheya,*" the "*Inipi,*" the "*Sundance.*" Everything is important to us, and no part of it should ever be taken lightly by anyone.

No one should insult or show disrespect toward anything related to the Sundance or native spirituality. Amazingly enough, there are so many people who go to one "*Hanblecheya,*" and suddenly feel they are experts at it. They see one Sundance, and they are experts at the Sundance.

Through invitation, they see and participate in a Sweat Lodge. Then the next week they are at their house, calling themselves shamans and building a Sweat Lodge, improperly, if I might add.

Most people don't even know the meaning of the word shaman. According to the 1994 Grolier Encyclopedia, the word "Shaman" comes from tribal groups in Siberia, where a shamanistic religion dominates the tribe. It has nothing to do with, and should not be used concerning native american culture or spirituality.

These people are running their own Sweat Lodge, and charging money for it. We don't understand this, it's wrong and only brings bad medicine to those who participate. Our spirituality is not for sale to anybody at any price. That people would even consider profiting off our ceremonies is disgraceful to us.

I don't want to pass judgement; the Creator can take care of that. Often people act out of ignorance, or their intentions are good. This we realize. However, it's time people were made aware of what they are doing to our spirituality.

People should understand that when they do a Vision Quest, or a Sweat Lodge, they are opening themselves up to the spirit world. We also believe strongly that there are good spirits and bad spirits.

We might call them spirits. We might call them medicine. There are bad energies out there, and people have to understand that they leave themselves wide open to this. They shouldn't be messing with things they don't know about. Besides that, it is sacrilegious to prostitute another man's spiritual beliefs. We don't appreciate it, yet so many people are doing it for sheer profit.

After messing around this way, they call me to help them out of what they bring on themselves. Some say that they feel snakes in their heads. Others say that they can't sleep because spirits are hitting them and keeping them awake for days at a time.

Then they expect someone else to help them. One person told me someone's spirit guide took their spirit guide to another planet! When we try to give them advice, they either don't want to hear it or never believe it.

This whole experience made me aware that I had stepped into a spiritual world that is there to benefit and help to the fullest. There is no limit. I can be helped, I just have to believe, show respect, and pray. The rest will come naturally.

As the old saying goes, action is the fruit of

thought. So when you think of something, it will come true if you, pray for it. A prayer is no more than a thought going from you to the universe or to the Creator.

The problem of the young man coming off the hill was straightened out when the Sundance Chief David, came back. He counselled the young man. He didn't condemn him. He didn't hold it against him for what he had done. He just told him, he shouldn't have done it.

I always say the Creator is not there to hurt us. He's only here to hold us to our word and serve as a spiritual foundation for us.

Wednesday afternoon we went out to get the sacred tree for the Sundance. When David said that we were leaving for the tree, the people pulled up their cars to get in line for the procession. As we pulled out, there were a dozen cars in line. We drove an hour to the turn off. Then five miles off the highway along rough and dirt road, to where the tree stood.

After cutting it down, we carried it on our shoulders until we got it to the flatbed trailer, and tied it down. People were sitting all over and around the tree holding on to it. Protecting it from any harm. It was so beautiful.

A mile and a half from where we had cut the tree down, we saw this friend of ours. His name is American Eagle. He and another gentleman were walking way ahead of us. Suddenly this great big bull stood in front of them. It was a Hereford bull, this guy was big. He stood looking at the procession of cars and the pickup with the tree. He was pawing the ground looking at us.

I could almost read his thoughts, "What in the world are they doing on my turf?"

American Eagle and the other old timer were out

there ahead of us. They walked toward the bull. American Eagle was carrying his medicine staff. He shook it at the bull. The bull was irritated, he started pawing the ground as though preparing to charge. Luckily we were close enough to the two elders.

David yelled at him, "Hey, American Eagle. You better leave that bull alone. He doesn't know you're carrying your medicine stick with you. You'd better get back in the pickup before he hurts you."

It was fortunate that we got there when we did. The two old guys got in the pickup. The bull, intimidated by all the cars, the tree, the truck and all the noise, trotted off. He certainly hadn't been afraid of two old timers getting closer and closer to him, almost threatening him. We all had a good laugh over that, but it wouldn't have been funny if something had happened.

So, anyway, it was beautiful because as we drove down the highway, with the tree on the trailer, people, most of them strangers, would get off the road. They stopped their cars to allow the tree to go through because it was a sacred tree. This didn't happen just once. We passed several pick-ups, cars, and vans, everybody slowed and stopped on the side of the highway.

We got the tree to a couple hundred yards from the Arbor, and stopped the trailer. Everyone gathered around the tree. As one, we picked it up and put it on our shoulders. This tree measures about thirteen to fourteen inches at the base, the large end.

It was green and very heavy. Slowly we start moving. The walk was slow and dignified. Although many of us are struggling, we are all quiet. As we carry the tree, we had to make the traditional four stops before we got it into the Arbor. Remember this was not my Sundance, but as a guest I'm also obligated to help in any way I'm able. I was just there to see my friend Lionel.

After getting the tree into the Arbor, we finally were able to lay it down. Inside the Arbor is all sacred ground. It's the only place the tree can touch the ground. Other guys had stayed behind and had dug the hole right in the center of the Arbor. It was deep enough to support the tree.

While the tree is laying there in the Arbor, many prayers are offered to it. We thank it for giving its life so we could have our Sundance. We let it know it was going to become a sacred symbol for us.

Everybody who was going to dance and pierce had to tie their ropes on then. They stretch their ropes out to different areas of the Sundance Arbor. When everything was ready, we started pulling the tree up with all the ropes. We were pulling to the west side to get the tree up. We pulled it until it stood by itself.

It had all these flags and colors, and offering flags made by many different people. When we got it up, all of us moved around, we formed a circle around the tree to keep it straight up and down. The other crew of men got in on the bottom and started burying the base of it.

They tamped it down good so that even a strong wind couldn't blow it over. When it was finally standing proudly, it was late in the evening. Everybody had their ties up and ropes on the tree. They were all ready for the next day.

The tree ceremony was over.

It looked like everybody was happy and ready. You could sense an intangible feeling of joy in the air. It was dark when we were through, and slowly everybody started disbursing back to their own camp. Everyone knew that morning comes very, very early.

I returned to the camp with my brother Lionel. David, Bernice and Al were sitting around drinking coffee, they were having supper. We joined them and ate too. After everyone was through eating we all sat around the campfire visiting. Tired and ready to hit the sack by this time I decided to go to bed.

Next morning as I got up, put my clothes and shoes on, I heard somebody yelling, "ho! Sundancers, let's go. It's 4:30, its time to get up. The sun is almost up."

Of course, he didn't really mean that because the sun was still two hours off. We always have to get up that early so we can go and do a Sweat Lodge purification, then come back to camp and get dressed. There is so much that goes into this beautiful ceremony.

As I sit here thinking about it, I have a little hollow feeling in my stomach. I really miss it. It has become such a big part of my life.

I still got up though I wasn't going to Sundance with them. I had my own Sundance to go to. I was just there to help my brother Lionel, and I had done that. I went over to the Sweat Lodge area. I didn't want to sweat that morning because I had to leave later and wasn't sure when I was leaving, that day or the following day.

Anyway, I went over there to see if anything was needed, found out nothing was, so I returned to camp. I still hadn't had my first cup of coffee, and they had a fresh pot on, so I followed my nose to it.

After my coffee, I returned to the Sweat Lodges again, to see if I could help. They already had guys designated to pass all the hot stones into the Sweat Lodges.

I felt sort of lost and left out. It was strange not to be in the Sundance. I kept asking if anyone needed my help. One guy asked me to help him with his Eagle whistle, and I did, I helped him get it going again. Another guy asked me to help him finish his ankle and wrist bracelets. It felt good to be asked for assistance. It had really been a problem for me that morning, finding something to do.

Everybody was happy to be there. It was such a friendly atmosphere. Everybody's feeling energetic, although a little cold, and it is so early in the morning. The energy is high, it is such a fantastic feeling. This is the first day of the Sundance. Even the smell about the place was invigorating. The smell of burning wood, the sage and cedar filled the air. It was burning in the Sweat Lodges. You even get faint whiffs of the hot steam coming out of the Sweat Lodges. It feels and smells so warm, and so cosy. Its difficult to explain, fully, all the good feelings associated with the Sundance. Especially this one, because it's so small, yet wonderful.

As things progressed I saw the guys going in and out of the Sweat Lodges. They came out and they returned to their camps to get ready. Everyone was ready with their beautiful colored regalia on, skirts made out of shawls. I watch in awe, as everybody is getting ready. I am thinking, next week I've got to go through this at my Sundance.

It is an honor and privilege to be accepted by all the people there, because I am an elder, and I'm there to help a brother.

Slowly, they get in line. They look for friends they want to be next to during the next four days while they suffer. They want be next to friends for support. By being together they magnify this energy. This powerful energy comes to every Sundancer. You want to share your energy with others. Others want to share with you . . . it's beautiful.

Finally, I heard the Sundance Chief again. Sheriiii-Sheriiii . . . He blows on his Eagle bone whistle. He is blowing it and telling everybody, "Get ready men, get ready, we are going in to pray." The line starts moving forward as the drums starts, slowly at first. Gradually, the beat picks up. It's the "Going In" song. You hear it playing across the Arbor over on the south side. It sounds so beautiful. The drum has a healthy, deep, mellow sound.

As they move around the Arbor, they make the traditional four stops to honor the four directions. A couple of Sundancers hold cans that have hot coals burning inside. They keep putting cedar boughs in the cans, the leaves are smoldering and smoking. The smell is wonderful. It's a purification smoke.

They follow each other around to the left. They are dancing. Everybody who is dancing is supported by brothers, cousins, aunts and uncles.

Many campers are gathering around the Arbor, to see the procession of dancers and people who have made the commitment.

From their first Sundance until the fourth, almost all Sundancers have a pipe, but they have not yet earned the right to do the ceremonies with it. The pipe is theirs but it is only in their care until they have finished their first commitment. After four years, they are a pipe carrier. They are believed responsible and knowledgeable enough to heal and offer blessings, all in the name of the Creator. We don't just take a pipe and say we are pipe carriers. Carrying the Sacred Pipe is a heavy responsibility. The privilege to help other people must be earned.

After everything is in place, the "Going In" song turns into the "Chanupa" song. The dancers all walk back under the Arbor, single file, as the song finishes. Ten to fifteen minutes later the drummers and singers start singing again, a Sundance leader stood up and said, "Ho-Ka-Hey . . . let's go. One more round, let's go."

The Arbor, the resting place for the dancers is not only to rest the physical bodies. It's also a place to meditate, to concentrate and pray for the things that you need, to think about the prayers you need answered. Some people, new to the Sundance think the Arbor is a place where the Sundancers relax and have their cigarettes. This is wrong, there is nothing to drink, nothing to eat, and in many Sundances they even ask you to give up your cigarettes. That is the end of all that for four days.

They start the second song. I'm in the background under the Arbor. I am there to dance with them and offer my support. I keep looking at all my brothers and sisters who are out there. They are suffering. They are going through a lot. I think, at least I'm standing on the outside. I can keep my shoes and shirt on.

As the day goes on, the sun starts getting hotter, and hotter. I think to myself, my God, how could they be taking it out there? I look at one after the other, to see how they are holding up. No one is complaining, or saying it's too hot or I shouldn't be out here. Humbled by the experience, everybody is honored for the opportunity to be dancing and praying for others. It's such an incredible feeling, standing there, seeing them suffer, without thought of themselves. Your chest swells up with pride, to be witness to this sacrifice, and to know you are one of them. This Sundance belongs to everyone there.

The day passed slowly, I could see the dancers starting to tire a little at a time. The heat reaches its peak, then the sun slowly starts sliding downhill to the other end of the horizon. Down to where it is starting to get a little cooler. Nobody pierced that first day, but it was an amazing day.

The Sundance Chief, being a good leader, had seen the condition of the dancers and let everyone know that it was their last song. Before they could come out of the Arbor, they had to do one more thing. They had the Pipe song, they picked up their pipes, then danced out of the Arbor. The Pipes are placed in a sacred lodge. That's where they keep all the pipes during the night. There was always a guard placed in front of the door so no one could go in there and disturb the pipes.

It was about six o'clock when they came in from the last round. Everybody started going into the Sweat Lodge. As they got ready, they dropped to their knees and quickly crawled in. There were three separate Sweat Lodges.

Everyone was happy as the day ended. Everybody danced, prayed and now it was time to relax for the night.

At the time, David allowed people to return to their own camp to sleep. He didn't have any tepees set up for the men and the women. This would have given the people who wanted to remain in the area around the Arbor, a place to sleep. So he allowed everybody to return to camp.

My camp was just my van. I parked right next to Lionel's tent, so I was close to everyone else. When I got there, they already had coffee and a pot of stew cooking. I got a bowl of stew and a cup a coffee. I savoured the first bite, rolling it around in my mouth. After going all day without food I was hungry. I took my time eating and drinking my coffee.

Al and Bernice, husband and wife, two of the elders there, they were about my age, had been dancing all day. Tired, sitting quietly, they talked and sipped their coffee. I sat close to them after helping myself to another. There were quite a few people there, their daughters, sons, Richard, Lionel and other people who I didn't know.

Quietly Bernice said, "Manny, you would honor us if you would dance with us one day, tomorrow."

I didn't know what to say for a minute.

Then I replied, "Bernice, I have my own Sundance to go to. I am honored you are asking me to dance, but I've got another commitment already."

"We know, we just want you to honor us, and dance with us one day. I've got to tell you something, Manny. This afternoon tired me out. The sun was really hot. Every time I looked and saw you dancing, it didn't matter that it was hot." She stopped, took a sip of coffee and continued, "Just the way you were dancing, your motions, your sincerity, helped me. The look on your face, really inspired me and kept me going, when I felt the most tired."

Al, her husband, looked and he nodded his head quietly. He says, "Me too, Manny. We would like you to dance with us."

Richard their son added, "Yeah bro', come on man, dance with us one day. Dance and suffer with us for one day."

When people offer you that much respect, you can hardly refuse such a humble request. At some point you have to consider their feelings, above your own. I had no choice really, but to say I would.

So, there I go again, forgetting tradition. I forgot it, in the spirit of the moment. When you make a commitment to Sundance, it's never for just one. It's a four year commitment. When they talked me into it, they talked me into dancing four years.

That wasn't their intention, I'm sure. It really doesn't matter because I'm committed to the Sundance as long as my health holds out, for the rest of my life. If I'm financially able, without jeopardizing my family, I'll Sundance from now on. It is nothing that I got talked into with my eyes closed. My eyes have been wide open every time I have made a commitment.

I felt wonderful that they should honor me in such a way. After agreeing to dance with them, I saw

Bernice get up and walk away. I noticed, but I didn't pay much attention.

A few minutes later she returned.

She said, "Manny, since you agreed to dance with us, I want to honor you with one of our shawls. This will be your skirt. I want you to honor us by wearing our family colors. Everyone that sees you in the Sundance will know that you are dancing with us and for us . . . for the Tail family."

It was such an honor, it choked me up and I thanked her.

I told her, "You don't have to do this. I've got my own shawl."

She says, "Take it, it's okay. You are going to honor us by wearing it."

Bowing my head respectfully I accepted the shawl. There was a chorus of glad voices.

Everybody was saying, "Alright, Manny, alright." Everybody was happy, laughing and smiling, shaking my hand and slapping my back.

I said, "I have to get a crown, ankle and wrist bracelets made."

Everybody jumped in to help. There was one guy on each piece. In five minutes they had them ready for me. They tied a couple of my small Eagle feathers on my crown. Suddenly here I was all ready to go into another Sundance that I had never thought of doing.

All I had come to do, was to help my brother Lionel through his Hanblecheya, his vision quest and the Sundance. This was his first Sundance. I wanted to see him off on the right foot. Now these beautiful people honored me.

So, I went to my van after everybody broke up and headed for their own blankets. I slept great considering, I was a little nervous about the next day. Only I knew what I had to do in this Sundance too.

Next morning I was up early. I went and did my traditional morning sweat. Afterwards, I headed back to my van and got myself all dressed up.

I was back at the Arbor when David got there. We talked and waited for the other guys. One at a time, everyone arrived from their camps all ready to dance. We started lining up. Everyone was in the same order that they'd been in the previous day. I got to fudge between two other guys who had been in the day before. It was a small Sundance and usually when you come in late, you always go to the end of the line.

It started slowly again, as it got lighter on the horizon. I could feel the little pins and needles from the mown down bushes. The ground was cool under the soles of my feet. It was such a good feeling to be there. The Sundance Chief started to blow his Eagle whistle, letting everyone know it was time to dance and pray.

Somebody yelled, "Hoka-hoka-hey, time to go."

The drums started, and again, I am reliving that incredible, feeling of entering the Arbor. Into that all healing, sacred circle.

We went through the first dance and greeted the sun. We prayed at the tree. We put our pipes on the altar facing the east, and we rested.

While we were resting there, I went to the Sundance Chief and said, "David, I want to pierce first round."

An incredulous look came over his face. He says, "Manny, you don't have to pierce."

Al heard me, and he also said, "No, no, Manny, you don't have to pierce."

Turning to face Al, "Al, David . . . you honored me by asking me to dance with you. Where I come from there's no free rides."

Al looked down at the ground almost as if sorry

at what he had asked me to do. They never even faintly thought that I might pierce for them.

I grabbed Al's hand and I shook it. "Don't feel sad, it is my honor to do this for you. I am happy that I can pierce for you and your family. Look at me and smile with me, brother. Laugh with me because this is what it is all about. It is about praying for each other, helping each other and knowing that you have somebody who is willing to suffer for you."

Al looked in my eyes and smiled.

He shook my hand and said, "*Ho . . . Washtelo . . . Wo-Pila.*"

David sitting in his chair, stood up and shook my hand. The man told me that if this is what I wished, it was a commitment between me and the Creator. "We will do as you ask."

They hadn't even prepared the paint to mark the chests with yet. It's not really a paint. It's a mixture of red dirt, clay and water that makes into a paint. A Sundance leader came over and they told him to wet the paint.

"Manny's going to pierce on this first round."

He went and got some water. When they painted my chest, the look on Bernice's face was filled with emotion.

She said, "Manny, you don't have to do this." She hadn't heard the previous conversation.

"Bernice, I have to."

She looked at me and she said, "You are my brother and I have to honor and respect what you want to do.

When the next song began, right away they started singing the "*Chanupa*" song. David went over and said something to them. They changed it from the "*Pipe*" song into the "*Piercing*" song. As we were going out, I stood right at the entrance of the Arbor where we do the dancing and praying.

It was as though a signal went out. When the *"Piercing"* song could be heard throughout the camp, people started coming to see who was piercing. The shade around the Arbor started filling up. Everybody went by, shook my hand and thanked me. I was thanking them, though not as individuals. In my heart I was thanking them for this day.

When they were finally all in, Richard, a Sundance leader came and took me right to the tree. After praying for a couple of minutes at the tree, I walked around and handed David one of my throw away scalpels.

I looked at David saying, *"Ho-Wana,"* meaning I'm ready.

I called Lionel to come in and be with me while I pierced. I laid down and they pierced me on both sides. I remember looking at Lionel's face. He had a look of pain and anguish. It's really hard. People go through so many strange feelings and sensations. It's impossible to describe the emotions that play across the face.

When you look at them, you see that those people are praying for you, and hurting for you. They care about my pain, about my blood and my flesh that I am giving up. I see it in their faces, I see it in their eyes.

After piercing me, I stood up and I moved back away from the tree. I started dancing. Almost everyone standing under the shade was now behind me, supporting me on that first dance. I danced and danced. Four times I went to the tree. On the fourth time after going to the tree, I prayed and I asked for strength and courage. I wanted to do this right for my new Lakota brothers and sisters.

I gathered up my rope as if I were going to lasso something in front of me. As I started moving backward, I let go one coil of rope at a time, I was going back faster and faster. Finally, as I dropped the last coil, it never made it to the ground. I was flying backwards faster than that coil was toward the ground. I hit the end of the rope. For that one split second of time, I felt like something had reached from the heavens and touched my chest, my face, my head and my heart.

The next second, I jumped up and yelled. I was happy to have honored these people. I was happy that I had done it with bravery, that I had succeeded.

That was the climax of the day. The day ended as beautiful rays lit the Sundance Arbor from over the mountain tops, as the sun went down. Everybody was happy, and jubilant. After the sweat, everyone shook my hand and thanked me for the dance. We spent the rest of the evening just visiting.

I told them, "Tomorrow I have to leave, but I'll be here in spirit with you. I will be dancing with you, every day."

Lionel smiled, "Will we see you next year?"

I got up early next morning. I went over there, and after they were in the Arbor, I said my goodbyes to everybody and left. I headed out of there and I drove south and east toward the Rosebud Reservation.

This was Saturday morning. Our purification started Sunday morning. So, I took my time. It's about a hundred and fifty mile trip.

A mile before I got to the mass grave at Wounded Knee, I could feel the restless spirits from that horrible time, asking me for my prayers. Every time I pass this area, I stop and pay tribute to all the men, women and children who had their lives taken so suddenly, and so tragically. Every time I stop, pray, burn sage and cry for their pain and the injustice of it all.

While driving, my mind wandered. I felt lost,

because I had left my brother Lionel behind. We were very close spiritually and I considered him a true brother. I was feeling lonesome, because of no one to talk with or share my thoughts. Maybe this was why I kept going from place to place. To have a cup of coffee, and someone to share conversation.

My thoughts travelled from one friend to another. Where could I go next? Who could I visit after the Sundance? I was always careful I didn't overstay my welcome. I was lonely, but afraid of rejection if I stayed too long. It's a terrible feeling.

The loss of my family had taken its toll on me, subconsciously, I was dealt a terrible blow to my self-confidence. I began thinking of my children again. To see them and talk to them would be the answer to all my prayers. One thought that always occupied my mind was, when am I going to see them again? I ached for the arms of my children around my neck.

When I got to Rosebud, I went straight to the little town of Mission and went in the grocery store. I replaced bread and canned goods that I had used at the other Sundance. Anything I might need for the next four or five days. I got some ice for my little cooler, and bought a couple of gallons of water.

Then I headed over to Rosebud Village. As I went through, I started seeing people I knew, people I had Sundanced with.

Our Sundance was on top of the hill, appropriately called, Ironwood Hilltop Sundance. Already people were starting to set up camps where they have been camping for years when they came to the Sundance.

I drove around, and I saw Emmanuel and Thomas from California. This was to be their first Sundance, and I was their "Grandfather." I knew they would make me proud.

There was one area, sticking out from the hill, south of the Arbor. We called it "California Ridge" because so many people from California came and camped there at the Sundance. I went there first. Setting up camp for me was just a matter of stopping my van. I was home.

I spent Wednesday morning getting myself ready and putting the final touches on my regalia.

In the afternoon, we headed out to get the sacred tree. Now this is a much larger Sundance than the one I had been to over at David's. There must have been twenty or thirty cars following the truck with the trailer to go get the tree.

Traditionally, what happens is this. Right then when you are cutting that tree down, the Sundance Chief selects another tree. He goes and takes tobacco to it, prays to it, and lets it know that it will be our sacred tree for the following year. There is more said to the tree, but only a Sundance Chief knows what he talks to a tree about.

We went to cut our tree down. Now this is going to sound amazing to many people, but it was right in the middle of a poison oak patch. I mean, we had to trample through poison oak. There must have been ninety to a hundred and twenty people. Every one of us went through it. Then we had to push it out of the way with our feet and our hands to get to the tree.

We had a young little girl take the first axe strike to the tree, and then a little boy. Two children who are pure of heart, spirit, soul and body to strike the first blows. Then they let the old guys like myself take a few swings. It's quite a sacred ritual. It's also quite an honor to be selected to do that.

Anyways, after the old warriors take their swings, then they let the young warriors go in there and chop it down real quick.

When it gets close to start coming down, they

push it, and all the young warriors get under that tree. Slowly, slowly they take one little whack at a time, until its resting firmly where it can't fall to the ground supported by all the men. When it was cut loose, we trampled out.

All that poison oak, and to the best of my knowledge, not one person involved in the ceremony, got a rash or anything from it. Now that's unheard of. You know, you can see two or three or maybe ten people being immune or not react to it, but for everyone to be like that? This is powerful medicine.

We were there for a sacred purpose. We were there to get that sacred tree that means so much to us. It's the tree of life.

We carried it up and put it on a trailer. Again as we travelled down the highway, people would pull off and stop. Those who lived in the area, knew the sacredness of the tree. They would stop as a sign of respect.

We must have travelled about ten miles, then we took it off the trailer. This time it was a larger tree, but there was a lot more people to carry it, so, it wasn't quite as difficult.

We made our four stops before we got to the Arbor. Once laid down, we tied our ropes on. This time I was there in time to tie my own rope on it.

Now is the time to mention this. In Porcupine, I went to David with my problem and asked him what to do. I told him that the spirits had come to me in a dream. They told me that I had to pierce every day of my Sundance. It would be for my children. I should pierce once on each side, every day for the full four days.

That scared me to death. When he consulted with the spirits and asked them if they truly wanted me to do this, the spirits answered, yes. That's what I must do so my children are protected. The one way to guarantee they will never be abused or mistreated, is to pierce every day during the Sundance.

I keep saying that "the spirits told me . . . " or they brought me a message. I'd like to explain how this happens. These messages always come to me through powerful and convincing thoughts. It feels as though the spirits enter my mind to make me aware of what they want me to do. Sometimes it can come as a dream. There's also "awake dreams" or "daydreams" that are just as powerful and real as any vision.

After settling down, I looked for Keith. I told him what had happened. We went into the Sweat Lodge together. He asked the spirits to bring him some kind of sign or word about what to do. Again the spirits came and said yes that is the way they wanted me to go if I wanted my children protected.

Normally they don't allow people to do more than one set of piercing. If they want to do two, it should be two in front and two on their back, while dragging buffalo skulls. If they feel they must drag buffalo skulls, or if they have made that commitment then it's okay. More than that in one Sundance they frown on it or they don't allow it to happen.

Keith told me, "You know, the spirits are telling you to do this. We should still go and talk to Norbert, and make sure that it's okay with him. He runs this Sundance."

They are trying to keep glory hunting people out of there. If someone is looking for glory, we let them know this is not the place to build their ego.

So, we went to Norbert and Keith told him what had happened word for word. What I experienced, what the other Sundance Chief had said, and what he himself had gone in and asked the spirits.

Norbert said, "Well if you made that commitment and they told you that, that's the only way to do it. You've got my blessing."

He went on, "I know that this will be a hard and painful Sundance for you. Not only are you going to feel the pain of those piercing wounds, but you are also going to feel the heat of the Sun, thirst and hunger. Another pain that you are going to feel is the pain of your limbs. Your arms are going to hurt, and your legs will ache. You will pay a heavy price for what you're asking. But you have the strength and the courage to do it."

So with that done, I started praying heavy duty. I prayed for the courage and the strength to accomplish what I had to do. Since I had already done one piercing, I told them that was the first one of my four days.

He said, "You only have three days to go then, because your commitment is to pierce four times, and you have already done one."

When we went in Thursday, I didn't pierce. I danced Thursday, and then Friday morning I was the first one. I pierced. I can't start to relay to you how hard it is to go through that much hunger, pain, and thirst. Along with the heat, and the constant blowing on my Eagle whistle, is very difficult. It took all the energy I could muster to keep myself on my feet.

The tiny little veins on the top of my feet started bursting. The whole top of my feet turned black and blue, like one big bruised club at the end of my leg. All those vessels bursting, along with all of the hours dancing in the hot sun, increased my suffering.

Pierced and pulling back on the tree, I smiled at Harold, a new Sundance brother I had met, from Pennsylvania. He was fast becoming a close friend, I had met him and his wife, Carlotta the year before, when we both pierced simultaneously.

I pierced Friday, Saturday, and again Sunday. By Sunday, my entire chest was inflamed, one whole mass of pain. Piercing ripped my flesh open every day. It was gratifying for me because I knew that every time I ripped my flesh out of my chest, one or more of my children were being protected.

Although not any single piercing was for any particular child, each piercing was for all of my children. I prayed that my children would come back to me someday, and be kept from harm. I prayed hard for this.

I finished that Sundance, my third Lakota Sundance. What a wonderful relief to complete it, and beautiful feeling. I hate to be repetitious, but I had found something that I really felt strongly about and truly loved. The Sundance will always sustain you. All you are expected to offer is belief, respect, and prayers.

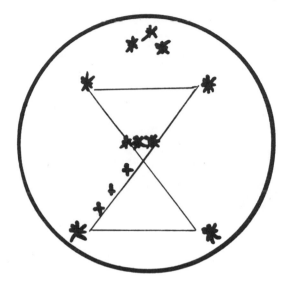

ABOVE - BLUE

"Star Path"
Orion's Lights

When I finished the Sundance that year, it made it my seventh Sundance. Since then, to the present, I have done seven more Sundances. I was dancing two a year. I had to dance at one to fill my four year commitment, and started another four year commitment at another one.

Something was happening to me at this point that bears mentioning.

Now separated from my wife, I was trying to get my life back together. While I was at the Sundance, my wife was processing divorce papers. I knew that something dramatic was going on in my life, but I couldn't quite put my finger on it.

When I left South Dakota, I returned to California. I got there to find a letter from the courts of Oklahoma informing me that on July 31, they were going to have a divorce hearing for my ex-wife. If I didn't appear in court they would take it as an indication that I wouldn't contest any of the court rules or terms they laid out. They would go ahead and grant her a divorce under those conditions. I am almost positive that she knew I wouldn't be there to receive the letter. She knew I'd be at the Sundance.

Of course, when I received it, it was a month and a half old. So there was no way that I could have made it on time or contested it. So now it was final. It was hard to believe, it had all happened so fast. I didn't fight for my children, because the very best I could ever be, was a poor mother. I figured, well, I can send them money. I'll learn to live with it. She was a good mother to them.

Soon after all of this happened, there were other things that kept bugging me. I kept getting reports that she was not treating them well. Although I don't want to get too much into this, I have to say their welfare concerned me.

This is why I was praying so hard that Grandfather would take care of them, and that no kind of abuse was to befall any of them. I was willing to give my blood, my flesh, and my pain to have my prayers answered.

I was really hurting when I found out the divorce was final. It didn't hurt me at all to be divorced. What hurt was to lose my children. I wondered what I was going to do without them. So much of my life focused around them, and suddenly I didn't have them anymore. I wondered what they were thinking of all this, and of me. I wondered if they blamed me, and what their mother had told them. I couldn't go to Oklahoma, not yet. I didn't know what I would do when I saw her. I felt it was better to stay away. I was still angry.

After that Sundance, I travelled up into northern California. Life was treating me really well. Everything I made I sold. It started to get late in the fall and I began to feel human again. I was sending the kids some money every week. Always sending money orders in their name, so they would know their dad was trying to take care of them, and was thinking of them. Much later, my son told me, "Mom said you sent us money in our name because you thought she couldn't cash it. She cashed every one of them and would give us $5.00 of it, then use the rest for herself or the house."

No matter what she did, she was a good mother, and a good wife to me for fifteen years. At this point I can honestly say I've got nothing against her.

I headed to Quartzsite, Arizona and sat in the desert for two weeks making dream catchers. At the time there weren't too many people making them. Those of us that were, had found it hard keeping enough made for the people who wanted them. After the two weeks, I walked into one store and they didn't even ask me the price.

The store owner said, "Manny, you've got dream catchers?"

"Yes, I've got a bunch."

"We'll take them all," he said.

It didn't surprise me, they are very, very popular. They were a good selling item. Naturally, I was happy and grateful that the Creator had given me such a great way to make money. Especially with high blood pressure, it was quite relaxing and not too stressful.

Now I had to head back to California and beef up my supplies of hoops, leather, beads etc. I had everything I needed, and started to make some more. I parked a few days out on the beach, and I stayed with a friend of mine in Torrance, California. I would park by their house, and sleep in my van. I'd ride my bike down to the beach then back to work.

I put myself on a minimum of at least ten dream catchers a day. It didn't matter what size or what color. I made them from five inch wooden rings, to eighteen inch rings. At the end of every week I had seventy dream catchers made. It wasn't bad for a guy living in his van with not too much overhead. Things were going good for me.

Winter came and went while in Torrance. I told my friends I wanted to head back to Arizona because in February, there's a big gem and mineral show in Tucson. It's the largest in the world. Every hotel and motel room in town is full. Many motel rooms become a retail and wholesale store for the exhibitors who fly in from all over the world. There's really nothing like it on earth! Some beautiful specimens, it's fascinating. You ask for it and someone's got it. It's also a great place for me to wholesale my crafts.

Headed in that direction, I thought I would go see my buddy, Emmanuel, in Julian, California. To see how he was doing. I felt lost. I didn't have a family and I didn't have a home. All these months on the road were starting to hit me, and the full realization of my situation was beginning to sink in.

My only concern was sending money home occasionally, and trying to make sure that they lived well. Of course, I didn't want to send too much because from what I heard, not all the money I was sending went for my kids. I heard some of it was going to support my ex wife's new drinking habit.

I didn't have a whole lot to be concerned with when I headed down to Julian. I had brought Emmanuel into the Sundance. He was a good friend.

When I got there, Emmanuel said, "hey, Manny, how are you doing?"

"I'm doing great. I'm just kicking back, making dream catchers."

"Well, look," he said, "I just moved into another house. This cabin is just sitting here empty." He went on, "If you want, you are welcome to stay here. The rent is paid for another month. There's a bed, color TV, a VCR, refrigerator and a shower. You can use it to make your crafts, you don't need to go anywhere. Get out of the van for a few days and stretch. If you want to stay longer than a month, I'll pay for another month, no problem."

How could I refuse? I thanked him and took him up on his generous offer. Right across the street is a working man's restaurant. Across the street from them was a video store that had over five-thousand different videos. What more could I want?

I would get up early in the morning. Go across the street and have breakfast. Come back and work, making five to ten dream catchers. Go have lunch, come back, make a few more, and then have dinner.

By then, usually, Emmanuel was around and we would go have dinner at a good restaurant in the area. I would watch videos at night. I was really enjoying myself. Local people would come over and say they heard I was making dream catchers up here. I would show them what I had and sell one here and there.

You know, twenty, thirty or forty bucks was pretty good, when you didn't have any overhead.

Suddenly out of the clear blue sky, something hit me. I'm sitting there, I'm making money, I'm making dream catchers. It's not costing me any rent. I mean, how much better can you have it. I was a little lonely, but not that much. I could handle that loneliness because I would get to talk to people, the waitresses and anybody around.

However, one Sunday morning I got up, walked over and had breakfast. I walked back to the cabin. Suddenly, I got this strong, strong urge that I had to get to Tucson. I have always been one to follow my intuitions. I've always been one to rely a lot on my senses and my prayers.

In a matter of minutes, everything changed. One minute I was completely at ease with myself with my place in life. Suddenly, the energy had changed completely. Something compelled me to leave as soon as possible for Tucson. It was almost as if I were running from the landlord or something. In a matter of fifteen, twenty minutes I was ready to go.

Just as I was finished loading everything into the van, Emmanuel drove up and said, "Manny, what's going on? What are you doing?"

"I've got to get to Tucson."

"But, you're all loaded up," he noticed, "you don't have to pay any rent here, you don't have to take off."

"Oh, I wasn't going to leave until I saw you,"

I said, "I just want to get there."

"What's the urgency," he asked.

"I don't know really, I just have to go . . . now."

"Well Manny, if you have to, I guess you have to. I'll miss you, you know, you're my bro. I hate to see you go. You were great company these last couple of weeks."

"Hey, Emmanuel, thanks a bunch. I really enjoyed myself, but its time to go. I'm really compelled to go to Tucson. Besides, in about a week or two some of my big customers from New York will be there, and I want to be there to meet them."

He shook my hand, and we gave each other a big old hug. I told him I'd see him later. A few minutes after that I was in my van and headed down the road. I took off down the hill, and it was about four hours later I arrived at my Mom and Dad's house.

Things had improved with my parents only two months before. I got in touch with my Mom before Christmas, and she asked me to come home and not to spend it alone. I told her that my hair was still long. She said, "Did you here that?" My Dad was on the extension.

My Dad said, "I don't care if your hair is down to the floor, come home, son."

Finally, my prayers were answered. When I arrived at my parents house on Christmas Day, my Dad came out to greet me. My Mom was crying with happiness that after five years her wayward son was finally home again. My Dad was happy to see me. It was the first time he'd seen me with long hair. He never made one comment about it. Later we visited one of my sisters. As we left her home I heard my Dad whisper to my Mom, "He doesn't look half bad with long hair, does he?"

My Mom turned and gave him a shocked look, not believing what she was hearing.

At least I was with my family Christmas Day. By now they knew that I was a Sundancer and what it's all about. My Dad seemed to have a new respect for me. He was hearing from other people about the Sundance, and how hard and admirable it was to be a Sundancer.

I spent that Sunday with them. The next morning I got up early. Mom wanted to fix me breakfast. I declined. Then she asked me if I'd stay a few days.

I said, "Thanks, Mom, but I can't stay, I've got to get to Tucson."

She said, "Why do you have to get? I've never seen you have to get anywhere."

"Mom, something is urging me to get there right away. I don't know what it is."

"Well, okay, you do what you want to do. I wish you'd stay a few days."

"I can't, Mom. Maybe on the way back."

I got to Tucson about noon that Monday, and I went to see this friend, Anna. She's a promoter, and promotes a big show there in Tucson. She had a big tent set up with booths inside and out. We walked around visiting.

She was busy, so I just left her alone and went my own way. I went to find a place to eat supper, then a place to park my van and sleep that night.

Little did I know that the next day, I would find out why I was driven to come to Tucson. It would prove to be a major turning point in my life.

Early next morning I got up and went into a restaurant and had my breakfast. Then I headed back to Anna's tent. As I walked around outside I ran into Nan and Dave, a couple of people I knew, who were set up selling.

We talked and visited for about an hour. I told

them I was making dream catchers.

Nan pulled me aside and said, secretively, "Hey, come here. Everybody's trying to make it on the native thing and trying to cash in on the dream catcher deal."

I asked her, "what do you mean?"

"Come here, I want to show you something."

So, we walked inside, and here's this short, little white girl. What does she have on her table? Nothing but a bunch of crudely made dream catchers!

Nan turned around and left, I stayed there. I started scowling at this girl, and she looks at me with her innocent, hazel eyes, and said, "Hi, could I help you with anything?"

I asked her, "Who made these dream catchers?"

She said, "A Choctaw lady from Arkansas."

"Well, true, authentic dream catchers were made by medicine men, not women."

Taken aback by my aggressive tone, I could tell she felt uncomfortable. She said she didn't mean to offend anyone.

She asked me if I knew about them.

"Of course, I know about them. I make them. Did you know that . . . " And I proceeded to lecture her on how it had been a tradition from ancient people and for elders to make them. For people who had problems sleeping. Now here's this white chick, from God knows where, trying to sell in my territory! Like I really owned it, you know.

She says, "You make them yourself?"

"Yeah."

"I'd like to see them."

Well suddenly this has turned from a lecture to a possible business deal. So, I'm all ears because business is business. I turned to her and said, "Well, I'll go get some."

She said, "I can follow you out to your car. My

girlfriend will watch the booth."

We walked out there, and of course, by now, I am trying to show off. I showed her all my dream catchers, big and little ones - all sizes.

"Oh my God, you made these?" She asked.

"Hey, I make all of them, and I don't need anybody's help."

"I'll tell you what, if you'll make them for me, I can sell these by the truck load!"

I looked at her, incredulously, but trying not to show it, "You can?"

She replied, "I have got connections in Canada like you can't believe!"

She was telling me that she was going to buy dream catchers by the truck load from me. However, I found out later she really was quite a courageous young lady. She would commit herself to things without a cane to hang on to, all the while trying to think positive. You know, the proverbial pot and window? Anyway, I had to admire her for her courageous and entrepreneurial nature. It was wonderful.

We walked back into the tent talking and making plans. My mind was in a whirl. I'm calculating how much money I'm going to make. I'm thinking that I'd have to get people to help me. I'd have to teach others how to make them etc.

I finally introduced myself to her. Her name was Melody. We both felt pretty good about meeting. I told her, I'm going to see these friends of mine, Thelma and her husband. They have a store in New York and Long Island. I want to go and talk with them to see what they need. I'd be back later.

So, I took off and found them. They did quite a bit of buying from me, in fact they bought me out. She asked me to make more before the show finished. They wanted to have some to take home with them. When we finished business, Thelma said, "Manny, we're having supper at Carlos Murphy's, you want to join us?"

I said, "I would love to join you, but I just met this young lady. I was going to ask her if she wanted . . . "

"Heck," Thelma said, "Bring her with you."

"You sure you don't mind?"

"Not one bit, we can just write it off as business expenses."

I said, "Great! Oh, but Thelma, I don't even know if she wants to go or not! I'll ask her and see what she says."

I felt pretty good. I had an invitation for dinner, I had met a nice young lady and my pocket was full from the sale.

I went back to where Melody was. I told her that I had to go over to the Post Office to mail my son some money for his birthday. It was February 12th, 1991. Then I had to try to find a motel room to take a shower.

She offered, "If all you need and want is a shower, you can go over to my motel room. There's nobody there, here's the key. Just bring it back when you're done. It's too hard to find a motel room in Tucson at this time."

Well, I'm a perfect stranger, but I guess she felt she could trust me. I found the motel where she was staying, and I went in and took a shower. Got all cleaned up, and left. This had taken me quite a long time getting everything done. So when I got back to her booth, it was almost time for her to close.

Although she never said it, I think she was a little bit worried that maybe she had given her room key to a person she didn't know. I think she questioned herself for being so trustworthy to a stranger. When I came in, I could see a look of relief on her face.

Then I asked her, "Well look I've been invited to this dinner tonight over at Carlos Murphy's. Do you have any plans? Are you going out with Darren and Sheila?" By now I had met her friends that she had come with.

She says, "Well no, they have plans of going some place, but I didn't want to go with them anyway. I'd love to go with you."

Thelma and her husband were already there. While we had dinner we visited and talked shop. We had a good old time and ate some fine food.

Anyway, we drove back to her motel room, and after parking our vans, we took a walk. We walked up the street. We went to a fast food place and sat just visiting. I felt stupid. Here's a fifty-two year old man, holding hands there like a teenager. I felt ridiculous, but it didn't feel out of place. We haven't been apart since.

I ended up helping her at the show. Then we left Tucson and went up to Flagstaff. We travelled around a bit, selling and making crafts and Melody said she really had to get back to Canada.

By now, I am deciding, I really love this girl, and I enjoy her company. I really hated to let her go. So, I thought well maybe, I'll go with her to Canada. If things are good, I'll stay, and if not, I can always come back.

It was quite an adventure going up there. We ended up at a "New Age" show there, which was quite interesting. It opened my eyes to many things that I hadn't encountered before. That show was the first introduction for me toward a new way of life and a new circle.

When the summer was getting into full swing, Melody and I came back into the states to attend the Sundance.

This was the first Sundance Melody had ever
seen. Just as her world had opened my eyes to many
things, the Sundance, which is my world, opened her
eyes to many different things. She saw how people
prayed and suffered for their beliefs. It made her a
believer in the native ways. Since then she has
accepted them and knows that it is a good way to
follow spiritually.

It's not just a matter of taking and taking.
Always when we take, we give, every time we give,
we take. Balance is always practised by the First
Native People. You see many signs on bumpers and
T-shirts say, "Walk in balance in this life," and signs
of that kind. We don't mean to walk in balance, like
walking on a tight rope. We mean walking in balance
with nature and with each other. It means respect for
everything, plants, all animals, our Mother Earth and
ourselves. Above all respect for the spirits, always
keeping that in balance. If you take the life of a tree,
plant two more because you are giving one of them
a chance of survival. If one of them should die, there
is still one to replace the one that you took.

People come from all over the world to attend
the Sundance, from the mountains of Peru to Europe
and Tibet. There have been a Japanese girl, Aztecs
from Mexico, Navajos, Danish, Tohono O'Odhams,
Apaches, Canadians, Germans, Afro-Americans and
even a Buddhist monk.

So there is no barrier. There are representatives
from all four races at different Sundances. The
Sundance flag is all four colors, representing the four
main races of people. That is why we say, "Mitakuye
Oyasin," meaning "All my relations," during prayer.
This is something that we share with our brothers. It
doesn't matter what color their skin is. We are one,
together on this planet. We should pray, dance and
give thanks to the Creator together. That's what

makes the Sundance so beautiful, so pure and so powerful.

We the Native American People, the Indigenous People, are the keepers of the Sundance beliefs. We're the teachers of the Sundance beliefs. It's our job to show others the way to our Spirituality. What we learn from our visions, we must share with others.

The first Sundance had been very special and inspiring for Melody. It had been on the Rosebud Reservation and she was quite overwhelmed and moved by the things she saw at that Sundance. It had been a tough one on her, because she was now five months pregnant. On top of that, the last doctor's report had been that we were expecting twins! Of course, it was a very intense ceremony to her. She met many of my friends I had been Sundancing with a couple of years, from California, Oregon, Maryland, and so many other places.

Two of Melody's friends even made a 1,500 mile pilgrimage from Ontario, Canada. Joe and Mieke came all that way just to pray and support us. Mieke is a very good psychic reader, and gets paid well for what she does. All the time she was there, she gave free readings to anyone who wanted one. Many Native People took advantage of her generosity.

Joe was busy in the cook shack, helping out, washing pots and pans. He was watching the front gate, as security. They gave up their time, effort and sleep to help any way they could. It was a big comfort to Melody having friends from home to hold her hand while she watched me in the Sundance. It was truly wonderful for all who were present.

This Sundance started just like all the others. The Sundance Chief followed tradition. We had sweats, we did our prayers and danced hard. It was a very special ceremony, for several reasons. The year before, I had wanted to pierce my back and drag buffalo skulls. I wanted to do it for my children. However, I didn't do it, because I had no one to help dress and take care of the wounds afterwards. This year, though, I had Melody with me. She told me she would care for my wounds. I didn't tell her what I was going to do Saturday morning, when we started the dance.

They marked my chest and back to indicate where I was going to be pierced, while Melody stood in the shade around the Arbor. She was crying, and holding Mieke's hand. When she realized that I had marks on the front and back, she knew something was up. I hadn't explained anything to her about dragging skulls, and no one else had dragged skulls yet. So it was a complete surprise.

Many non-native people believe that we worship the buffalo. It's not a case of worshipping the buffalo, but offering our respect. To us the buffalo gave its life for hundreds of years, so that we were able to survive and live. From there stems the respect that we offer it, because to us it meant abundance.

Also there is the spiritual significance of the buffalo. We strongly believe, that the buffalo brings us an abundance of spiritual energy so we can cope with everyday life and day to day realities. This is the reason that we pierce our backs and drag as many buffalo skulls as we can. The more there is, the more power we receive from the buffalo.

To feel the weight and pain that comes from dragging buffalo skulls, actually becomes something good and joyous, rather than fearful. You realize you are giving thanks in a special and sacred way.

This is also the reason that every year I make my piercing bones out of buffalo leg bone. I always give them away to people significant to me, that I love.

Anyway, I knew if I told Melody what I was going to do ahead of time, she would get upset, in her condition I didn't want her worrying.

When I went to the tree to pray, I untied my rope and stretched it out to the north west side of the Arbor. All my friends knew that was where I danced and prayed while attached to the tree, so everyone moved to stand near Melody. That Saturday morning, I was the first to pierce. After my chest was pierced, I was standing in my spot, dancing and praying. I looked across and I saw my friend, Harold. He had pierced right after me.

We danced back and forth to the tree, the traditional four times. On the last time, as I ran backwards, I saw Harold break loose, one split second before I did. When I broke loose, a Sundance leader took my wrist bracelet, and ran with me around the Arbor to the west side.

They had four buffalo skulls tied together waiting for me. They pierced my back and attached the four skulls. Using the sacred staff, I started slowly, moving forward. The pain on my back was immense. I gritted my teeth and started praying hard, asking for courage and strength. Stopping to honor each direction, as I reached it, I made one complete circle of the Arbor. On my second round, just past the north direction, the left piercing broke loose. I stopped, not realizing what had happened. I had felt a hard jerk on my back and some pain. The pain seemed to center itself more on the right side now, and I didn't know why.

My Sundance brother, Henry, danced next to me. He leaned over and told me, "Keep going, Manny, one side broke loose."

I leaned into the other side, thinking it might break loose too. It didn't, it was really hard pulling the skulls when you're out of balance like that.

I got them moving again, and continued around the Arbor until I had gone around four complete rounds. The right side piercing had held the whole time. Finally, I finished, it was time to break loose. I backed up to the skulls. A few of my Sundance brothers, sat on the skulls and I took off running. I hit the end of the rope and broke easily enough. Though still in pain, I was thankful it was over.

The sacred pipe that I had for five years was magnificent. It had been made with cut beads. The designs were geometric and it was fully covered. My ex-wife had made it. I didn't feel the same way about it anymore, it couldn't bring on the special feelings it had before. It was time to pass it on. I did some praying, and asked the spirits what I should do. The message came to me through thoughts.

Sunday morning, I didn't dance, because the two piercing had taken a lot out of me. I felt I'd fulfilled my commitment. Midday, I went to the Arbor, carrying my old pipe and another beautiful pipe I had just received from Todd, a pipe maker from Pipestone. When I got behind the Arbor, while the other Sundancers were resting between rounds, I called for Harold and Henry.

They were both happy to see me. As they walked up, they were smiling and laughing. Harold asked me, "What happened Manny, you feeling lazy today?"

I replied, "Come here, I've got something for you."

When they were standing in front of me, I presented my old pipe with the beading on it, to Harold.

He gave me a puzzled look, as though asking me, "Why are you giving me this?" He couldn't speak, he didn't know what to say to this gesture.

"Harold, do you remember saying to me that if

I ever wanted to get rid of this pipe, to give it to you? Well brother, here it is, it's yours."

Henry was getting upset, wondering what was going on. He asked, "What's wrong? Why are you doing this?"

Turning, I held up the other pipe to him and said, "Henry, its time for you to have a new Chanupa. Please take this, it's my gift to you."

They were both speechless and emotional. I could read their faces, they both thought that I was leaving the Sundance for some reason. They both had tears in their eyes as they shook their heads, as if to say, "No, Manny, you can't do this."

Then I explained to them, it was time that I had a new pipe to go with my new life. That I wasn't leaving the Sundance, I only wanted to honor my two Sundance brothers. Both looking at me, not knowing what else to do, they embraced me. All three of us shared tears together. It was a special moment for all of us.

We left the Sundance Monday morning, drove to Rapid City for a couple days rest, and much needed showers.

After we rested and recuperated, we left Rapid City. Leaving there we went down through the South Dakota Badlands, the road taking us straight to David Swallow Jr.'s Sundance. Because I had committed myself the year before, I had another three years with David and his people in Porcupine.

We were well received on arrival to the Sundance grounds. The people at that Sundance made everyone there feel welcome. I introduced my lady there, where she made a lot more friends. Here is where we met Arnie and Dee Dee for the first time, a nice couple from Colorado.

It wasn't very long after arriving that we had to go after the Sacred Tree. Melody waited back in camp. It was getting hard for her to get around and it was so hot. That was the main reason that she had remained in camp. She was preparing dinner while I went with everyone else to get the tree.

Everybody gathered behind David's pickup to follow him to get the Sacred Tree. The convoy continued until we pulled off the main highway. David pulled the pickup close to the edge of a river and stopped.

Opening the door, he said, "This is it, boys!"

I saw him pointing across the river. I thought to myself, "Can't we get any closer than this? How are we going to get the tree here?" Then I asked David the same questions.

He replied, "This is as close as we can get . . . and we're bringing it back on our shoulders!"

I said, "Oh."

Getting out, I looked back and people were getting out of their cars. David removed his boots before getting into the water. As I entered the water in my bare feet, I felt my connection with Mother Earth. It's hard to explain, the feelings I receive at times like this. A common occurrence suddenly becomes a very special moment in your life.

Something triggers your sensitivity, something happens to your soul. A soft, intense feeling of peace and contentment comes over you. I felt the warm water around my feet. I felt the cool, soft mud squish up between my toes. Both seemed to massage or caress my feet.

It was as though Mother Earth was telling me that the next four days were going to be hard on my feet. Still she wanted to show me that she also could be gentle on them. She wanted my feet to feel the gentleness first, then the other extreme. It was about a foot deep, but it was really wide, with a slippery, muddy bottom. After crossing over, we gathered around the sacred tree. We followed the tradition of cutting the tree.

Once it was down, thank God it wasn't very big! We placed it on our shoulders and began walking across the river. Everything went well, until we started slipping on the mud. Then it became very difficult to carry it without touching the ground or water. Slowly we made it across and started up the steep embankment on the other side. I slipped and fell, more than once, trying to get up the side. It was very difficult. Once when I fell, I used my body to keep the tree from falling on the ground. Finally, with strenuous effort, we got it on the trailer.

At a distance of two hundred yards from the Sundance grounds, we took the tree off. Some people put a cross limb underneath it. There were two guys on each side of the tree, carrying it like that. We walked, and carried it toward the east entrance of the Arbor. We made the four traditional stops so the medicine man could thank the four directions. The last stop was the longest.

By now everyone was hot and tired. It was getting to be early evening. Finally we took it inside. When we gently laid it down, it was with the thick end laying right at the edge of the center hole in the Arbor. Melody was waiting, along with many others. They had their prayer ties and flags that we were going to hang at the top of the tree, on the limbs. It was such a beautiful sight to see all those people walking up and saying prayers and tying all those flags on the tree. The Sundance Chief tied the traditional silhouette of a buffalo, a man and an Eagle wing securely to the branches.

They did that so the Creator would recognize the men who were praying. The buffalo was on the tree because of its sacredness to us, the Eagle wing represented the Eagle, so he would take our prayers to the Creator. The man represents all humanity. Sundancers started coming from all over to tie their ropes to the tree.

Things got quieter and quieter around the tree until everybody finished. Everybody was in there together. As one person finished, he stood in a circle away from the tree. Then other people would have good access to it.

Finally, the Sundance Chief, David announced, "Grab hold of your ropes we're going to stand it up."

We started pulling, then some men got underneath the tree, pushing it up higher and higher, until it was standing straight. It was so beautiful and majestic. When the leaves were free of the ground, people were still, waiting for the tree to stand erect before moving.

The only movement was the vibration of men struggling to stand that big tree up. When the tree was straight up, it was like a tension was broken, all the beautiful little leaves started flickering and waving. There was a slight little breeze that just made them dance.

The base of it went down into a deep, four foot hole. After moving it around and centering it, we had two or three guys start shovelling in the dirt. By now the only thing holding the tree up were the ropes. It almost looked like spider webs branching away from the tree. If it started leaning a little too far one way, we would pull the other way a little bit. It's such a magnificent sight.

Anyways, we got it standing up. All the dirt was right up to the top as they tamped it down. The tree was standing alone in all its glory.

As each man walked back up to it, he would find his rope and tie it down around the tree. They secured it to the tree, so they wouldn't be flopping around when we danced around it the next day.

Once the tree is up, there is a pause, as though everyone holds their breath a minute. It's so impressive and awesome to see this magnificent tree, and to watch it come alive, it takes your breath away. Now it could stand alone like it was before it was cut down.

Melody and I returned to the van. We had a light supper, then I took off my muddy, dirty clothes right next to my van. I crawled in, the blankets were sure a welcome relief. I must have been tired because morning arrived very quickly. It was almost as if someone had awakened me and said it's time to get up. It was early morning.

The next morning we did our traditional sweats and danced into the Arbor. It got hot very early that morning, but it was beautiful. Everyone was in great spirits. This was Melody's second Sundance in two weeks.

After we greeted the Sun and placed our Sacred Pipes on the Altar, we retired to the dancers resting place. We were all just sitting around visiting and introducing ourselves to dancers we didn't know. It was a good time to meet new brothers. It is a good time to encourage all the new Sundancers, to help overcome their nervousness and fears. We do a lot of joking, but to some people it is a very scary thing.

Before the Sundance started, Al managed to get a buffalo for the Sundance. He had it butchered, so he kept the skull. He had the skull laying back behind the Arbor.

Al asked, "Lionel, do you want that buffalo skull?"

Lionel looked incredulous, "Really? Yeah, I really like it, and it would look good in my living room. Sure I'll take it."

I looked at Al and then at Lionel. I said, "Al you're giving Lionel that buffalo skull?"

"Yeah." Wondering what I was getting at.

I says, "And you accepted it, right Lionel?"

"Yes, I am very grateful. I was secretly hoping this would happen."

"Well Al, you realize what you have just committed Lionel to, don't you?"

A look of surprise and confusion crossed their faces.

Then Al began to understand what I was talking about, and he got this, "Oh no!" Look across his face.

"That's right Al," I said, "You gave it to him. He's accepted it. Now he's got to pierce his back and drag that skull."

Al explained, "I knew all this, but when I gave it to him, that is not the way I meant it."

I went on, "I know, and I realize you didn't do this to hurt him. I don't want to see him go through any pain, but that's the traditional way. He's got to earn the right to have that buffalo skull in his home."

Al looked at Lionel and said, "It's true Lionel, I'm sorry, I forgot."

Lionel said, "Oh, man. Things are really serious around here!" Then he laughed, "If I had known that, I could have picked one up for $50.00 at the trading post!"

Everybody busted out laughing.

This other old timer listening to all this says, "Hey Lionel, I'll drag it for you for $50.00!" He says, "I'll pierce and drag it for you, you give me fifty bucks and you can take the skull home!"

Then this other guy jumps up and he says, "I'll do it for forty!"

Then I tried to lighten up the moment some more and said, "Well, I'd do it for twenty-five. I don't mind piercing."

Everybody was laughing and making a big joke

out of it because it had been so very serious at first.

Then Lionel quietly asked, "Do I hear twenty?!"

Another round of laughter started. Now everyone was laughing uncontrollably.

Finally, after the laughter had died down. Lionel says, "Well Al," as he shook his hand, "I accepted the skull. If I have to pierce for it and drag it, I'll do that."

Al said, "You think he should do it now?"

"It doesn't matter when Al, as long as he drags it. You gave it to him, it's up to you when."

Reluctantly, Al says, "What I mean is, it's really getting to smell bad, and it has been dead for three days. It still has the hide and everything on the skull. It hasn't been boiled or anything."

"Actually, it might be better this way," I said, "It's green and heavy. If the Creator wants him to drag it around all four times, Lionel will remember it well. If the Creator doesn't, he'll break loose before dragging it far."

They decided to wait until the following year for Lionel to drag the skull. He wanted to drag a skull that didn't smell so bad.

The dance continued all that day. Later that afternoon Lionel came to me with tobacco, and said, "Brother, I would be proud if you would do the piercing for me."

This was quite an honor. Also I had never pierced anyone before. His asking made me emotional. I took the tobacco, and said, "Yeah, I'll do it for you, I'd be honored, brother."

When you go to an elder to ask for advice or a favor, you always go to them with a tobacco offering. Sometimes, when you don't have a bag of tobacco, you can use a cigarette, that's the traditional way. If the elder isn't committed to something else, he almost can't refuse to do the bidding.

So I explained to Lionel, "Whenever you take tobacco to an elder, first tell him what you want him to do. Before you give him the tobacco, give him the opportunity to refuse. If it's something he can't or doesn't want to do, that gives the elder the option of backing out if he wants."

They started singing the piercing song. We placed Lionel where everybody could shake his hand as they went out of the rest area into the Arbor.

I took him to the center tree and said, "Lionel, it's going to be a good one. It'll be okay, don't worry little brother."

He smiled nervously, "I'm not worried."

I let him pray for a little while. I went to David and explained that I might have to put my glasses on. He told me to tie some sage on them, so the spirits will accept it.

In recent years my eyes have been getting bad and I need reading glasses for anything up close. Yet when I brought Lionel to the buffalo hide and laid him down, he handed me his scalpel to pierce him. I closed my eyes as I put my hands on the tree. I asked *"Tunkashila"* to give me compassion and to guide my hands. I asked for better vision so I could see what I was doing.

Suddenly, when I opened my eyes, my eyesight was better than ever before. As though the brightness of the sun had increased, tenfold. The whole world just brightened up for me.

When I knelt down next to Lionel, I was on his left and David was on the other side. David did the first piercing on his right side. I held the flesh while he did it, and then inserted the cherrywood piercing stick through Lionel's flesh. While David was tying the rope on, I grabbed and pinched the flesh together. David reached across to help me hold the flesh up. I took the knife and slowly slid it into his flesh. I felt a slight little pop as the sharp pointed scalpel broke through the flesh and then another pop as it went through. I didn't want to hurt my brother Lionel any more than I had to.

Slowly, slowly, I sawed and pulled the blade to my left to widen the hole that I had made. Blood sprang up immediately through the wound. It was hard to see what I was doing. David took Lionel's piercing stick, and put it through the wound. Immediately we knew the wound wasn't big enough.

Shaking his head, David indicated that it wasn't big enough, to cut some more. It would tear out if we tried to push it through his flesh. David pulled it back out and I inserted the knife back in and cut a little bit more. Slowly, ever so slowly I cut down, until the opening was about a half inch in length. Then David grabbed the piercing stick and pushed it through the cut, through the wound that I had inflicted on my brother's chest. This time it slid through easily.

I looked at his face and it was expressionless, just a little pale. I know the pain he was going through. I felt this pain many times in the past, but I also knew that he was a warrior. As I tied his rope on, I made a figure eight around the wooden stick. Now done, we picked him up.

I shook his hand and said, "Brother, you're on."

He was in pain and shock. I could tell by the look in his eyes, they had a dazed look. So I kept him moving and talking. After a few minutes I could see that he was feeling better.

Lots of people can't take the pain and the shock that accompanies the piercing ceremony. Many guys have trouble accepting an injection at the doctor's office. This is under the hardest conditions possible, but you know, this is a traditional way. It may be crude to other people, but to us we are doing the very best for that person, the best we know how. We do it with the Creator's blessing and with as much compassion as possible.

I helped Lionel with his rope. I was trying to take it easy on my little brother. I knew that he was in pain and hurting, but I also knew he was there by choice. Nobody ever told him he had to be there. I also realized he had found his spirituality, his road, and he was quite happy and content with it. This is what makes the Sundance so wonderful, no one ever tells you that you have to be there.

As Lionel backed up, his rope was tight. I told him to breathe deep and pray hard, the harder he prayed, the less pain there is.

I kept telling him gently, "Pull back and stretch that flesh. The more you stretch it now, the easier it will break when the time comes. Pull it back, I told him. It hurts, I know, brother, it hurts. Pull it back."

He pulled back until the rope was taut. It was bouncing and stretched tight. His chest was way out of proportion. I said, "Ho ka! Come on, go to the tree, and pray brother."

He danced toward the tree, then knelt on the ground and prayed. The tree becomes such an important part of us. It becomes God, in our eyes. Only this way we have something to touch, to pray and cry with. He got up.

Lionel was pulling back stretching and stretching. The pierce on the right side suddenly popped off. He looked at me with surprise, I was standing right next to him.

He said, "It fell off, it broke loose!"

"Hey, that's good brother. Now you only have one to break loose. The spirits are smiling on you. Be grateful, be grateful that they are smiling on you. They are trying to make it easier for you. That's good."

He smiled at me, "Hey, alright." He was stepping lighter now, and with more vigor.

By now he had been to the tree three times. I told him, "this time when you go to the tree, on your way back, run hard. Don't worry about it, I'll be here to catch you."

David waved him to the center. David runs that Sundance and controls when people go to and from the tree to pray when they are piercing. So he waved him on. We went with him right to the tree.

"You are ready to break loose. You only have one side to break," David softly spoke to him giving him words of encouragement. He would be breaking loose soon.

I saw David wave his fan at Lionel telling him to break loose. I couldn't believe that little guy could run as fast as he could. He turned around and he was coming really fast from the tree. Just as he hit the end of the rope, I was standing two feet behind. He started to fall and I grabbed him. I caught him under the arms and picked him up.

"All right brother, you're loose."

He was so happy. "Manny, I did it."

"You bet, brother, it's done."

I led him around the Arbor back to his place, and everybody was touching him. Everyone wanted to feel his energy, that tremendous amount of energy given to a Sundancer when he pierces is so beautiful and contagious.

One afternoon, Melody was very tired and decided to lay down in the van to rest awhile. She had burned herself out, from so many days of dancing, first over at Rosebud, and more dancing at Porcupine.

Slowly, she climbed into the van. Leaving the doors open, to catch any little breeze that might happen by, she stretched out to rest. The weather was hot, and though uncomfortable she started to doze off.

After sleeping awhile, she woke up and could hear the drums. Suddenly, she felt something move. It was her babies, moving for the first time. Then she felt it again and it was the thrill of her life. They had started moving inside her, she got up and couldn't believe it. She was so excited that she couldn't restrain herself. She started to cry, wishing she had someone there to share her miracle. She got up, came over to the Arbor and asked me to come over to where she could talk to me.

"What's wrong?" I asked, worried. I was confused because she was excited, but she was also smiling.

She whispers, "Guess what honey?"

Worriedly I ask, "What's wrong?"

She says "The babies moved. It's the first time, they were listening to the Sundance drums and started moving." Then she continued, "I've felt it move a couple of times already. It almost feels like they start dancing every time they hear the Sundance drums."

Naturally, I was thrilled. It was such a beautiful thing to happen. It was such a special thing to happen at the Sundance.

The first movement a child makes, is in response to listening to Sundance drums. I can't think of anything that could be more wonderful to happen to a person. I believe that where a child is, when it hears its first sounds is important. That the sounds were of drums beating is also very special.

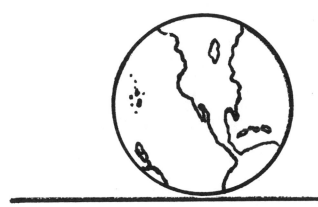

BELOW - GREEN

"Mother Earth"
Giver of Life

After the Sundance was over Melody and I headed back to Buffalo, New York and Niagara Falls where we had a storage shed. We kept some of our crafts there because of the difficulty in taking them across the border. We would stay in a motel for a few days and make plenty of crafts. I'd call customers and if they placed an order over the phone, we would make it, then go and mail it to them. They would send the money orders to Canada. So, it was a pretty good thing all the way around.

We continued doing shows and selling our crafts all over Canada. So, as life went on, things got a bit easier for both of us.

Once we were getting ready to do a show at the International Center. It was a big, New age, psychic fair. In fact, this is considered the largest show in Canada, if not North America. We were to set up that morning when the phone rang.

We just started renting a three bedroom house there in the little town of Richmond Hill, just north of Toronto. The call was a friend of mine from Oklahoma.

I asked him, "How did you get my phone number, Bob?"

"It wasn't easy, I called all over California! My friend, are you sitting?"

"What do you mean?"

He says, "It's about Vivian. She got killed in a traffic accident last night."

We were separated and divorced for awhile now, so it really didn't bother me emotionally. I felt absolutely nothing against her. If anything, I still felt some anger toward her. My first thought was how the kids were, and I asked Bob about them.

He said, "They are fine, just fine. They're here at my house. What do you want to do about them?"

Still in shock, I tried to gather my thoughts and said, "Look, I don't have any money right now. I have a four day show starting tomorrow. If you could watch them, I'll pick them up after the show."

He says, "Okay, wire me permission to accept responsibility for these kids or the Welfare Department is going to come in and take them. If they do that, when you get here, you will have a real difficult time trying to get them back. By then, they would have them placed in foster homes."

I pleaded with him, "Don't let anyone touch my kids, Bob. Please, keep them altogether for me. I appreciate your concern and your friendship. I'll call you when I get ready to go."

I thanked God for Bob's intervention, and prayed I had a good show. I was able to do consultations and give advice. I did exceptionally well considering all I had on my mind. You really find out about "friends" at a time like this.

Now is a good time to tell about the world Melody introduced to me. The first time we went to Canada, we went directly to a psychic fair in the little town of Kitchener, Ontario. We got there a day late but still got our things set up in record time.

I saw things in there that I didn't know existed. I saw some pretty weird individuals at that show. I tried to act as though I saw that sort of thing all the time. Melody just laughed at me. She knew I was uncomfortable around some of them. It really opened my eyes to new things, that I understood but not in the way I was seeing it there. We saw things like UFO abductions, palm readings, astrology and more.

After that introduction I was telling Melody about how our people have been consulting the spirits for thousands of years, to give us guidance. Some old

Medicine People used different methods to help people. Some used feathers, sticks, small bones and even stones. Some men or women, would use the "hands on" way of healing and helping. Much of it was done by drumming and singing while they contacted the spirits for advice.

So this is not a strange world for some of us First People. Its just that we don't have a name for it, that I know of. A good native friend of mine, Ted, calls himself a Seer. He does "readings" for people and I heard he's very good at what he does.

For myself, its something I've had all my life. I always had people asking me for advice and telling me their problems. It seemed I always had words of comfort for them and knew what to tell them in their time of need. I helped a few friends of mine resolve their problems, when they were ready to break up.

I did this for years, in fact, all my life. It was so much a part of me I didn't realize that I had that gift. It is a wonderful gift. I'm very grateful for it. I just didn't know anyone would be willing to pay me for the advice I had to offer. I was so wrong. People pay counsellors, consultants etc. for advice everyday. They pay for advice and the time that person offers. It's really no different.

The Creator brought me a way to help people and feed my family. It's a fair and good exchange. That's what my Melody showed me. I now know that I am a seer, interpreter, advisor, and counsellor and very good at it. Now I have a great deal of experience and have testimonials of predicting peoples future's and advising them on how best to use that advice. I'm proud to be a part of this old and honorable practice. I thank Melody every day for helping me to realize my gifts and use them.

So when we were in our greatest need, out of the blue, our friends Barry and Carol called and asked if they could give us some money. Another friend, Georgina offered her financial gift. Then a new friend that I had just met, Ted, gave us money to help. Then Carl, Shawna and Melva offered their financial help. This generosity from everyone really choked me up. There wasn't words to thank them. I was very grateful, and thanked the Creator for bringing me such special people in my time of need.

It is hard to give everybody credit who deserves it, because so many people deserve credit. People I didn't even know, came from everywhere to help us. Everyone who gave money gave it unconditionally, without strings or a time limit to pay it back. Without their help, I don't know how we would have done it. It was a lot easier to get my kids.

Right after the show, Melody saw me off at the airport in Toronto. After everyone's help and what we had earned, I had gathered $3,000 to take with me. By evening I was in Tulsa and my friend Bob met me alone and took me to his house.

When I got to Bob's house, my children were there waiting. My twin girls, Mary and Becky, just had their tenth birthday. The accident happened right before their birthday. Some friends of the family, Barbara, Mildred and Sherry bought them a couple of little presents. I was very grateful.

Seeing my kids for the first time in two years was a very emotional time for everyone. I had missed them immensely and done many prayers for them. I pierced for their protection and safety. I prayed to get them back some day. I sure didn't expect it to happen this way.

This is why the spirits told me that I had to dance and pierce every day for my children the year before. They were trying to see if I were worthy or willing to sacrifice for my children. My red chest was swollen, inflamed with pain, and burned from so many piercings. I was dancing and praying for my kids, that they would come back to me. I had four girls and a boy. I prayed God would protect them from any sexual, physical or mental abuse. I asked him to do whatever was necessary to keep them from harm. God also knew that if they were with me, I would make sure they were protected in all ways.

I strongly believe the Creator warned their mother to stop what she was doing. My kids were neglected for some time. Their mother left them alone long periods of time. There were transient people staying at the condemned house they lived in. Perhaps, the Creator warned her some way, and if she didn't stop, drastic steps would be taken to protect those children. Now if indeed, my prayers led to what happened to her, I certainly didn't mean it like this. Prayers are powerful tools, especially when you, pray for children.

Although the kids didn't like the over protection from everyone, I hoped that one day they'd understand. It protected them from the so-called friends and neighbors, from the gossip and stares and their pointing fingers, until I got there.

I did all this to prevent difficulties with the child welfare offices of Oklahoma. I picked up my children and took them away from all that. Even if I wanted more clothes for them, there was no way I could get them. All the so-called friends of my ex's, went through their house like tornadoes.

They took all my guns, silversmithing tools, clothes, chainsaws - everything, all the things that we had together, even the kids' clothing. I can't believe how people acted like vultures going through the house. Luckily, some friends who used to work for us, were able to save a few of the real personal items that belonged to my wife. Things she wanted to leave the kids. That was good, and I appreciated it.

All this time I had a sick feeling in my stomach. Wondering how I was going to deal with all this, with my kids back in my life. How Melody was going to handle all the kids, when she was pregnant for the first time. Though Melody said to bring them up and we'd manage, how would it be when reality set in? Her mother didn't want her to take on that responsibility. Melody had no experience with children at all, she'd been an only child.

All these things were going through my mind. Wondering how it was going to change all of our lives. My heart would ache for my children, every time I thought about how their whole world turned upside down, overnight. How they must feel to be suddenly in the care of a dad they hadn't seen in two years. To find themselves with no home, no mother, no clothes and no creature comforts. The only thing they had to hang onto was faith in their dad. I felt so, so sorry for them over their losses and confusion. They were all clinging to me, to protect them from the storm in their lives.

Anyway, I picked up the kids after buying a car. My friend Bob took me down to a little town, Claremore, and we bought a station wagon just the way it was sitting in the car lot. I didn't know if it had a good or bad engine, transmission or anything. I knew absolutely nothing about it. In my state of mind, the only thing I could do, is depend on "*Tunkashila*," God, to help me. So, I bought the station wagon, put the kids in it, and left for Canada. I hadn't even been there twenty-four hours.

On the drive, all the kids wanted to sit by me in the front seat. Almost as if the back seat was too far from me. I was all they had now. The first stop was that evening in Joplin, Missouri. We stopped at a motel room, and all the kids took showers. We stopped at a store and bought them two new sets of clothes for each of them. After everyone dressed and cleaned up, I took them out to dinner. It was as if they couldn't eat enough! They were so thin and undernourished looking. I wondered what their life had been like while I was gone. It still breaks my heart just thinking about it.

We worked our way slowly, steadily all the way up to Canada. When we reached the Canadian border, of course, Melody had undergone a big change in her life.

She had taken the house we rented and turned it into a home for all the new arrivals. She found bunk beds for all the kids, mattresses, sheets, pillows, pillow cases. It was quite a job for a woman who was seven months pregnant. By now she was that far along. You know, it's a big job for anybody to come from an only child type family atmosphere to five children that she had never met before. They ranged from fourteen to six years.

It was quite an adjustment for her, yet she did it very admirably. I've been very proud of her and always thanked God and the spirits that brought her to me. It seemed it was all in preparation for this. She needed someone in her life, and while in Tucson had prayed for someone to share her life.

Her strong prayers called me from California. I came because the call was powerful. It was almost as if God knew that eight months later, I was going to need her. I was going to need her for my kids. I will never forget the day when I called her from the border and I told her we were coming. Our friends Barry and Carol were at the house to greet us. Melody cooked a big turkey with all the trimmings.

When they walked in, except my oldest daughter and oldest son, the three younger girls greeted Melody with open arms. They called her "Mom," which meant so much to her. She was crying and hugging them. She was loving them and loving that she was getting all these children. She used to say in the past that she always wanted a large family.

I told her, laughing, "You didn't expect them all in one day, did you? At least you didn't have to change diapers, by getting the children like this."

"No, but I have quite a bit of love to give them, Manny."

Anyway, it wasn't long she had them all registered to go to school. Which was a pretty difficult thing to do in Canada. Thanks to the sympathy of the school board for what had happened to them, they overlooked some red tape so my children could be put in school. I am very grateful to the school board for all their help.

Another big event took place that should be mentioned. Melody and I got married! My son, Rockie gave her away at a civil ceremony. All my daughters stood up with us, and they were just beautiful. They were all stunning. I was very happy about it. Although she was eight months pregnant, I wanted her to be legal when she gave birth.

Perhaps the plans for the wedding and adjusting to Canada, helped the kids keep their mind off the trauma they had gone through. I think it made them feel more secure in their new home and environment. We had a wonderful reception at Melody's mother Lynne's house. There were many tears and laughter.

It also bears mentioning, when the kids arrived, friends from everywhere came to help Melody get ready. Bags and bags of clothes arrived everyday -- clothes, shoes, toys, books everything they could possibly need. It overwhelmed me the generosity of people. News travelled fast about what happened to the children, and everyone was so great.

They missed a bit of school, but not much. We adjusted to our new lives as best we could. We spent that winter attending school functions and the library became a large part of our lives, because of Melody's influence. We didn't have much of a social life anyway and visited the library often, though sometimes the cold weather kept us home.

December 20, 1991. . . All day a fine snow had been falling. The temperature wasn't very cold, but the air was crisp. Early that evening, Melody fixed supper and we all enjoyed it, sitting around quietly, visiting and eating.

Suddenly, Melody said, "I don't feel too good, I think I'll lay down for awhile."

I asked the girls to get the kitchen cleaned up, for mom. Melody called me from the back bedroom and said, "I'm feeling a lot worse, honey, I'm having bad cramps."

We called the hospital, and they suggested a warm bath, and a beer, to make her relax. Which she did. However, the pain was getting worse and worse, so we called the hospital again. Now Melody was laying down and the nurse asked to put her on the line. When she talked to Melody and described the pain, the nurse told us to bring her in, that she was in labor! They said they'd be ready for her.

When I told my son, Rockie that he had to stay with the other girls, while my daughter, Stormy and I took Melody to the hospital, Rockie freaked out! He was like the proverbial, "cat on a hot tin roof!" It was really funny to watch. It wasn't as though he hadn't been through this before, with four younger sisters. I guess this was different somehow.

I knew I was in trouble when I stepped out the door. There was about six inches of fresh snow on the ground. Our driveway had a slight incline and was hard to get out with snow. I shovelled and cleared it as best I could. Stormy helped Melody get ready. It was hard for her to walk, but we got her in the car. I still had trouble getting out, and worried that we might get stuck in our own driveway. Again, Grandfather looked after us and we got out.

We headed to the hospital. By now it was snowing really heavy, the flakes were large and wet. The wipers were having trouble keeping the windshield clear. If you've ever been in a snow storm like this, you know how tricky it is to drive and how hard it is to see. The hospital was about eight miles from where we lived. It took about half an hour to get there, but seemed further.

In the hospital, the nurses waited for us and took her directly into the labor room. My daughter Stormy and I went in and stayed with her throughout her labor. She arrived about eight in the evening, and was in labor for seven hours. We heard that wasn't very much for a first birth. To me it felt like days. It hurt me so much to see my Melody in so much pain. I wished there was some way I could take it from her. Stormy was helping Melody breathe and holding her hand through it all. This was pretty amazing, as Stormy was only thirteen years old. She had the responsibility of all the kids when her mother was gone.

At 3:07 am, December 21, our baby girl arrived. We had found out a couple of months before that there was really only one baby, not two as we had thought for so long. She gave birth so fast Stormy ended up holding one leg, while I held the other. The delivery was completely natural. No drugs, no cut, the baby just arrived. It was such an incredibly beautiful thing to see. I have fathered eleven children in my life, and this was the first one I ever saw being born. What an amazing sight it was. It happened so fast, the doctor wasn't there. Only two nurses were there to help her deliver. The doctor arrived at the end to cut the umbilical cord.

This was a big accomplishment for Melody. She was having her first child at thirty-four and we were concerned about her health. I prayed for a healthy baby at the Sundance the summer before. She turned out beautiful and perfect in every way. I made a commitment to Grandfather, to pierce my back and drag buffalo skulls to thank him, if he brought her to us in good health and complete. She is a wonderful addition to the family. It took that little baby's energy to unite us as a family. The kids instantly fell in love with her, the new little sister.

Melody has made such a big difference in my life. She's introduced me to so many things. I've changed a lot because of it. I'm not as angry as I was before, and I'm more tolerant. Seeing our child being born was such an amazing experience. I thanked Melody for allowing me to witness such a wonderful event. We named her, "Oriona," (Or-ee-on-ah) after the constellation Orion. Her middle name is "Estrella," which is spanish for "star."

They took Melody upstairs to a room with the baby, so Stormy and I left. It was about four in the morning. As Stormy and I walked out, the first thing I saw on the ground, was three small snow sparrows, pecking away at some crumbs on the hospital steps. The spirits had brought me a name for my little daughter. Her native name is Little Snow Sparrow.

After Melody and the baby got home we all settled into a routine controlled, of course, by the whims and temperament of the baby.

Spring was upon us before we knew it. We started thinking of the Sundance. It was getting time for me to go and give thanks, to show my appreciation for all we had received the whole year.

The Sundance season arrived and we got ready to go. Money just appeared, it seemed, when we

170

needed it. We bought a little pop up trailer that sleeps eight. We loaded up that car that we had from Oklahoma, and we went south. Across the border to Niagara Falls we took our time. We camped out along the way going toward South Dakota.

This trip was really special to me. Although my children attended all four Shoshoni Sundances in Wyoming with me, this was their first Lakota Sundance. It was quite a special event for all of us because they were going to see things that terrified their mother. So we travelled along, and stopped in Pipestone, Minnesota. Once I had a quarry there and I would quarry out pipestone.

This is the place where all the native people hand craft the sacred pipes. Commercially, there are many versions of "peace pipes" sold in different places. However, a pipe from Pipestone, Minnesota, has a card stating its authenticity, and they are only made by native people. This is where I buy my pipes to take to the Sundance. Sometimes I bring several and give them to the Sundance Chief, so he can give pipes to those Sundancers he deems worthy. The giving of a pipe is very important, and something to be thought about very carefully. When the Sundance Chief gives a pipe and makes someone into a pipe carrier, the Sundance Chief becomes responsible for whoever and whatever happens with that pipe.

Traditionally you can't buy yourself a pipe, it must be given to you. As I've mentioned before, to be a pipe carrier is a sacred responsibility, and not to be taken lightly.

We met with some of our other friends coming from Maryland. It was a wonderful time. We went down to the quarries, and saw Todd, Ray and other guys I knew who are carvers. They make pipes, quarry the stone and do the actual carving of pipes.

I also would mention, I will not buy or sell any

part of the Eagle and will not sell a sacred pipe. There is quite a bit of dissention about who's right and what's wrong. I personally believe a pipe is just an object, just like anything else, until it goes through ceremony. Many tourists buy them at the center at Pipestone.

I don't believe a pipe should be considered a sacred object until it has been in a Sweat Lodge and has had a medicine person breathe life into it. When it is given the breath of life, the power to cure, then I believe it would be sacrilegious to buy or sell that "Chanupa" or pipe. Because of the fact, that now it is a living entity, you don't sell people, you don't sell living beings.

I believe that the ones who have been there for generations quarrying the pipestone are the only ones who should be able to sell those pipes. It's a gift given to them by the Creator. This is the way they feed their families. In the old days although they didn't sell them, they used to trade for ponies. They traded for pemmican or dried buffalo jerky. They traded for deer skins or beads. Everything that was tradeable, traded for Pipestone. So, if anybody is able to sell it, I think it would be those people. These are the only people from whom I will buy a pipe. I will, if the occasion arises and the trade is fair, I will trade for a pipe. As far as I am concerned, that is acceptable and makes me happy. I don't have to please other people.

After meeting the other Sundancers, we headed toward South Dakota. Before we got there, something remarkable happened. One of my girls, Rebecca, who was ten years old at the time, told me, "Daddy, I want to Sundance. I want to be in there with you, and share. I want to experience it."

I sat and had long talks with her. My son Rockie also said he would like to be in the Sundance with me. It humbled me, my two children honoring me like this. That they should choose to follow me in the Sundance and the way of the "*Chanupa*," the Red Road. We sat and talked and I asked them questions, to understand why they wanted to do it. I felt their answers were appropriate, so I allowed them to dance with me. I also explained that they had to dance four years before they really made up their minds about piercing or not piercing.

I think my son was glad of that. He felt he wasn't ready for piercing yet. He just wanted to be with me in the Sundance.

We got to the Sundance and there was quite a controversy because it had broken apart, and our Sundance grounds had moved to another place. It was at Hollow Horn Bear. They gave permission to Sundance on their grounds, until we found a permanent place.

The year before, I asked the Creator to give me a healthy normal baby. If my prayer was answered, I committed myself to honor the Creator and my baby. I would pierce my back and drag buffalo skulls. Though small, she was still bright eyed and bushy tailed, looking at everybody. She was very alert and aware for only eight months.

Now was the time to fulfil my commitment. The Arbor in a Lakota Sundance circle is not big. But it's a long way around if you are dragging buffalo skulls. It happened just as I asked.

Melody told me after, that when people around the Arbor realized that I was going to pierce, at least fifty people ran, to stand behind me, and my family. It was as though everyone knew something special, was about to happen, and wanted to be a part of it, and to support me.

First I pierced in the front, once on each side. When I broke loose, and danced around the Arbor,

I immediately returned to the Sundance Leaders and asked that they pierce me on my back. When I was getting pierced, I asked Lessert to make this a special piercing. I did not want to break loose until I had done my four turns around the Arbor.

He said, "Okay, it's up to you." When he finished, he leaned close to me and whispered in my ear, "Manny, that's guaranteed to hold 'til Christmas!" He had made the piercing deep.

The reason I had to instruct him to make it a good piercing is that sometimes they don't want to hurt you so they don't pierce too deep. Guys break loose before they have done what they came there to do, because of the weight of the skulls. I wanted to make sure they pierced me deep enough so the flesh wouldn't break before I was finished.

While standing there being pierced, my mental state was high. It felt good to be giving back something, for all the Creator brought me. Henry came and stood in front of me to give his personal energy, and support. He looked right into my eyes and held both of my biceps with his hands. He watched to see if I was alright. Would I faint or something, did I have the courage to see this through and looked in my eyes, as the blade cut me.

After Lessert pierced me, he said, "Ho-ka." He smiled at me, "Okay, Manny, you're alright."

They tied me to the buffalo skulls. I was fortunate, I believe, because there were only four skulls, and they only weigh twenty to thirty pounds each, although they can get pretty heavy.

I asked for my baby daughter to be brought to me, I told them, "I'm going to carry her around with me."

They brought little "Oriona," to me, my Little Snow Sparrow, and I held her in my arms. It was quite a sight to see. Here I am an older, dark and tanned, native man. Here she is, a little wistful thing, a little blonde dressed in a white outfit for the ceremony. At times I call her my little jelly fish.

They gave her to me and I started dancing. It felt so wonderful, the experience of carrying my child who God had given to me with all her limbs, and as normal as any child could be.

Melody explained to me after, as best she could, what was going on while I carried the baby around.

First there wasn't a dry eye anywhere. Men, women around the Arbor, even some Sundancers were crying. My girls, Stormy, Dory and Mary were crying and holding on to each other. It must have touched people's hearts to see a man suffering for his daughter. It was more than that, people got emotional because maybe they felt I was carrying a part of them. As though the baby represented every one of the people who witnessed this special ceremony.

True to my request and true to the friend who pierced me, both places where I had been pierced hung on as I danced around the circle. I could feel the gravel under my feet. I could feel little breezes. I could smell sage. I started slowly from the west and stopped first to the north and I held my baby high to the spirits of the north and then continued.

When a Sundancer is pierced in the back and is dragging the skulls, he has to lean forward, sometimes almost parallel to the ground. The weights behind him are heavy. As the skulls tumble around, they land on their forehead and their teeth. When they hit their teeth, they just dig into the ground and this yanks the person backwards. When this happens, the pain is excruciating.

I danced on. I offered her to the east and when I got to the south I offered her to the south. Each time I stopped and offered her to each direction, it was really difficult to get started again. Usually, when dragging skulls you are given a sacred staff for each hand to help pull you along. However, when I took the baby and was offered the staff, the Sundance Leader said, "You're not gonna need this," as he took it out of my hands, as though he knew I would have the strength to pull without it. Finally, I went around and stopped and I offered her to the west.

When I describe offering the baby to each direction, it is offering her for a blessing from the spirits. When we do the smudging ceremony and burn sage to purify ourselves, we offer it to each direction as a sign of respect to the spirits.

I was yanked back and forth, back and forth. I started moving forward. I started going a little faster. I felt so good, but I was fast tiring out. My mouth and my throat were so dry, yet I still felt good and full of energy. I felt as though I was putting the whole world behind me, yet I felt like I had the energy of everyone in the Arbor helping me pull and helping me push.

The baby was quiet, looking around, she'd play with the feathers on my Eagle wing fan a little bit. She had my fresh blood all over the white outfit she wore, from the two pierces on my chest. Melody wanted to keep the outfit, so one day she could explain to the baby what it was all about.

I went around my second time, I was catching my breath. I started going around the third time, and I felt really, really strong. I believe the baby gave me energy. The support of everyone watching and praying for me gave me strength. The courage from the Creator, all helped to keep me going on.

Everyone was feeling my pain. As I reached the west side of the Arbor the fourth time, they stopped me. I thought I had another time to go around the Arbor. They said, "That's it, Manny. You have gone around four times."

That's the tradition. I stopped. I was feeling very exhausted, very dry. My heart was pounding. I wasn't perspiring because I was dry.

Now it was time to break loose. Someone took the baby from me, and then Henry said, "Okay, Manny its time to break loose, its time for you to break from the skulls."

This big friend of mine from Olympia, Washington, a red-headed, freckled faced Sundancer, Don, says, "Manny, I'm with you, brother. What do you need me to do?"

I asked him to sit on the first skull. Smiling at him I said, "Hang on, Don, I'm going to take you for a ride." Smiling in return, he didn't answer, just turned and walked toward the skulls.

Then my children, Rockie and Becky, sat on the second and third skulls. What they were doing was anchoring the skulls so that I could break loose from them. After everyone was in place and ready, I stood back as close as I could to the skulls. Way up in front, another of the Sundancers was standing there waiting to catch me when I broke loose.

I took off running at a full gallop. I was running fast and low. I wanted to make sure that I broke the first time. If a person doesn't break the first time he has to try again and again until he succeeds. It's very painful to try again. At the last instant, right before I broke loose, I looked over at the man who had pierced my back. He was standing there looking, but not at my face. He looked at my back, and as I broke loose, I saw a look of surprise on his face. He was surprised that I had broken loose as easy as I had.

I've got to tell you something. It's not easy to break the flesh. It's very, very tough. I've seen guys who were pierced, the flesh holding the pierce together has been a quarter of an inch across. Yet I have seen those guys try to break three, four times before they can break loose. It is amazing how tough and resilient our skin is.

This is why I always tell people when they are Sundancing and they are piercing, I tell them to pull back, pull back, stretch that skin. It makes it easier to tear later. It's also how seriously you view the piercing ceremony. To realize that it's not to be taken lightly, or a macho thing. To pull back is to show your willingness to suffer. Once you are pierced and hooked up to the rope, the only way to get off is by tearing it out.

So, the look on his face was pretty incredulous when I broke loose so easy. I suppose I make it sound a lot easier than it was when it happened. I had fulfilled my commitment to Grandfather. I had carried my baby around four times, as I asked the Creator to help me do.

Since my job was done, I had done it with honor, respect and many prayers. The Great Spirit saw no reason for me to be hooked up to those skulls any longer. So, he allowed me to break out pretty easy on the first try.

We finished out that day with much joy and good wishes from other people. That day was a long and hot one, but a good one. It had been hard on me.

At this Sundance they allow everybody to return to their camps. This tradition changes from Sundance Chief to Sundance Chief. It depends on how he wants to run his Sundance, whether you can return to camp each night. Sometimes, you have to stay in the Arbor the entire four days and nights. At David's Sundance, he asks everyone to stay in, unless they must leave for medical reasons.

When I got back to my camp, it was still not quite dark. Many people were visiting each other here and there, talking about the day. I sat by our camp, with the sun behind us. We had our little

trailer and were sitting in the shade. This other
Sundance Chief, my good friend Keith, had come to
support me. He sat and my girls brought him a cup
of coffee and a sweet roll. He sat there quietly, had
his sweet roll and his coffee.

"Manny when are you coming to my Sundance?"
He asked quietly.

"Keith, I've got another Sundance to go to right
after this one. I'm doing this Sundance, then I have
to go to the other one, that asked for my help."

Disappointed, he continued, "You could do the
same with me. You could come to help us. I would
really like to have you there. You've got powerful
medicine."

Well, I started to be swayed, because he was the
man I felt so good with the first time I did my
piercing. I was getting persuaded to go with him. I
thought of all the controversies that I heard of
surrounding the Sundances.

There are mixed feelings, egos and politics
involved now in some Sundances. The Sundance is
becoming accepted with people from all over the
world. There's bound to be conflicts of interest, with
so many, from different cultures and beliefs.

Conflicts occur, especially among the Native
people, there is arguments about whether to accept
these outsiders or not. It's only been the last few
years that outsiders were allowed in. In some
Sundance circles, they want to keep it a Native
American ceremony, exclusively. Again, it depends
on the Sundance Chief.

Although I'm not a Sundance Chief, I do have
my own opinions. I've been to the tree enough times
that I feel that I can express them. Some Chiefs allow
outsiders into their Sundance, to dance and worship
with us. Yet others don't want anyone except Native
or First Americans in their Sundance. Then there's

some Sundance Leaders that don't want anyone except Lakota (Sioux) dancing in theirs. I've heard some say, "We don't want any white people, or we don't want any Mexicans here." I'd like to ask them, "What is a Mexican? Isn't it a mixture of European and native? What is the blood lines of the so called full bloods?"

I'm sure that if there are any pure bloods left, there's very few. The biggest percentage are mixed whether we accept it or not. That doesn't make us love "*Tonkashila*" and the Sundance any less than the other so called full bloods.

Then there's the matter of money to run the Sundances. Who has the money to give us so that we can have a Sundance? The white people do, we certainly do not. They are the ones willing to help us and all they ask in return is to be allowed to pray with us. Granted, there are people that use our way to profit and abuse our spirituality. "Grandfather" can handle them. We can't blame all of them for the acts of a few. They don't like to be categorized, either.

I would like to quote one Sundance Chief, Norbert, "The Sundance flag has four colors in it. It doesn't belong just to us, it belongs to everyone who is willing to honor, respect and sacrifice for our beliefs. If anyone is willing to learn, we should be willing to teach and not to judge other people by their color."

During my talk with Keith, I explained that I felt I had committed myself enough for this year. Possibly in the future, I would Sundance with him.

Keith gave me a message that the spirits told him to bring me. They told him because of the way that I Sundance, and how often I've pierced, now I was ready to help people. I would be given two special stones, as a way to help people. They would not be crystals or anything similar to that, just ordinary stones, but special healing stones with powerful medicine in them.

This was ironic to me because, unknown to Keith, I made a good part of my living making an item called, "Stone People Medicine." The creation of these small stones were also brought to me in an unusual way. I am happy to say, our family has lived very well from the Stone People, and are now selling them all over the world. What Keith was telling me seemed quite a coincidence.

Anyway, Keith told me I would know when they came to me, it would be under such unusual circumstances that I would know.

"Manny, I don't know why I am saying this to you or doing this. I was told to do it, so there it is."

I replied, "Keith, I don't know anything about healing. I wouldn't know what to do or say."

He says, "No, none of us do. We all have to learn. When it comes to you, you will know and you will be shown the way. The same way you were told to come to the Sundance, and pierce. You will know what to say, what to do. It's going to be very good for you. Remember it's not you doing it, it's the spirits helping you do it. With the stones, you will help people."

Here was the message that the Spotted Eagle had given me in the Shoshoni sundance. That I will be shown how, and when to help people. Just as the Eagle had given me the message was brought to me by a medicine man. This message could not come from a stronger source. I have to believe this Sundance Chief's message was from the spirit of the Spotted Eagle.

I have always had problems with words like healer, healing and things related. There are too many people claiming they can heal, sometimes with profit being the only intention. So I use the words carefully. This was told to me by a Sundance Chief who received the message from the spirits. I believe it wholeheartedly. Neither of us has any thing to gain from this, because there is never any charge for spiritual healing of this kind. I never hold out my hand for money for what I do.

It is also known once you have suffered at the Sundance, when you have done it for four years, you have earned the privilege and the right to give blessings to people. Always offering it in the name of the Creator. To cleanse houses, cleanse people, give names, whatever people ask for you to do, you can do. You have earned the privilege, and the right.

We left the Sundance. My brother Henry from Maryland was having a Sundance two weeks after that. I told Henry that I couldn't make it. He asked me, "Come over, I really need you."

I said, "Henry if I can, I will, and if I don't, it's because I'm not supposed to be there."

We headed south to Oklahoma so my kids could see some of their old friends. From there we went to Arkansas to see Melody's friends, Darren and Sheila. Then on to Memphis, where we stopped in for breakfast with dear, old friends, John and Betty.

Something very interesting occurred after breakfast, at John's house. He took me aside and told me he had something for me. It was my first sign, from what Keith had told me. He honored me with a beautiful, smooth stone. He explained that he knew I needed it for something, he wasn't sure what. It was quite an honor and exciting to receive this gift so soon after being told it would come to me. I hadn't seen John in years. He knew nothing about what Keith had told me, yet here he was giving me a stone. After giving it to me I told him everything. He just gave me a knowing smile.

Then we headed north toward a Pow Wow in

Ohio. I was honored when they asked me to do the blessing of the grounds. I did it in an unusual way, I used four veterans. I put one in each direction to guard that entrance. When the prayer was over, I brought them back in. It was a beautiful little ceremony. It was a fantastic Pow Wow. We were there for three days.

While I was there, another interesting occurrence happened to me right there at this Pow Wow. A non-native woman set up next to us, and she approached me with a gift. She gave me a stone. She explained that she'd been carrying it for about two months, and didn't really know why. She had picked it up at a Sundance in Northern Ontario, Canada, near Manitoulin Island. Her son had been at a Sundance and while there she was told by the spirits to bring this stone with her. She had no idea whom it was for or why she was bringing it, but she was told it was for someone.

When she presented it to me, she felt good and became very emotional. She knew that it belonged to someone else, and it wasn't hers. Her only job was to carry it to the person that it belonged to, which she realized the minute she saw me. When she gave me the stone, I was immediately reminded of what had happened at the Sundance. I knew instinctively that this was the second of the two stones I had been waiting for.

That's the way things happen when you are in this spiritual world or are communicating with the spirits. The spirits create this drama, so you remember that it is not you, but them doing the healing. They teach you how to use the stones in the right way. It might seem unusual, but it is very real.

Right after the Pow Wow we stopped at a campground. We checked our messages from home, and found out one of our customers from Baltimore had called and said she needed a bunch of our things. When Melody returned the call, she took the order, and it was quite substantial, good enough for us to drive there to deliver it. We still had a couple of weeks before the kids had to return to school.

That way we could visit my Sundance brother, Henry, and some of our friends who lived over in that area. Melody was happy to go there, because she knew that Henry's Sundance had been the weekend before. So she didn't mind driving there now.

When we got to Baltimore it was very hot and humid. We got a motel room and just kicked back for the rest of that day. The next morning we went out to our customer's store. During the conversation with her, she mentioned, "There's a girl I know that always dances at Henry's Sundances. She told me that they're getting ready. In fact, they start today."

Today, was Thursday. Henry's Sundance was moved to this weekend. I looked at my wife.

Melody said, "I can't believe this. It was supposed to have been last weekend."

The store owner said, "It was, they changed the date for some reason or another, I don't know why."

As a joke on the way there, I had said to Melody, "Oh, this is the weekend for Henry's Sundance."

Melody laughed and said, "Oh no it isn't, it was last weekend, honey."

Understand, that she did not want me to Sundance again, because of my sunburn and this would be my second Sundance. It was getting a little hard for this old man. So, she was pretty sure it wasn't that weekend, yet, here we are receiving verification that it was now. It wasn't when we thought it would be. When we found out about it, we called on another customer, then headed out to Henry's place, because that's where the Sundance is.

When we got there they were singing and dancing. They'd gone in that morning. He had quite a crowd. When Henry and Harold saw me, they were very happy. We all got emotional. Here I was, needed and I didn't know it. The spirits had again manipulated my life to take me where I was needed, and where I had to be. After that greeting and everything by everybody, I told them, "Look I've got my trailer over at a camp ground. We'll get here early, and I'll dance with you tomorrow."

Everybody was really happy. Melody was a bit upset, because she knew it had been Henry's prayers that had brought us here. She was worried about my health and condition from the other Sundance.

That evening, while we were having dinner together, Melody dropped a bomb on all of us.

"Honey," she said, "I'm going in to Sundance with you tomorrow. I want to be there with you and for you."

We both started to cry, I felt like the whole dining room had gone quiet, I couldn't hear anything. It was the last thing I expected to hear from Melody. Once, shortly after meeting in Tucson, Melody said that if there was ever a time I couldn't Sundance for health reasons, she'd go in my place. It humbled me, that she would consider going through it. My daughter, Becky also wanted to go in.

The next day, we brought our trailer and set it up at Henry's. We went into the Sundance later that morning.

They took us to a Sweat Lodge. We entered from the east and started Sundancing. It was wonderful to have Melody there, and Becky again. This was a small Sundance, but a good one.

The day before, we saw a young native man, Jim, lying on the ground suffering since the morning before with a severe migraine headache. Melody had asked me to try to help him.

I said, "No, it's not time. He's paying some kind of karma or he's suffering for a reason. It's not time. If he's like that tomorrow, I'll help him."

When we went in, I saw Jim again, still very sick. I went right to him.

I told him, "Come on, get up."

He says, "No, I can't, I'm too sick. My head hurts bad."

I asked him to come into the Sweat Lodge with me. I called some others, to make four warriors, we took him inside.

I did what I was supposed to do, although at first I didn't know what to do. I was just leaving myself open to receive instructions, directions from the spirits and they showed me what to do and I did it. We were in the Sweat Lodge about a half hour. Coming out, all of us took Jim and laid him back down where he was before.

He lay there for about half an hour. During a break, I went over and visited with some other friends. Not long after, Jim, came up to me. Understand, he had not moved for two days. His eyes were as clear as could be, where they had been full of pain and anguish before.

With a big smile, he said, "Manny, I want to thank you for doing whatever it was you did. I don't know what kind of medicine you have, but it is good. You're gonna help a lot of people."

He shook my hand and went back to his spot under the Arbor. He was really grateful and I was surprised that I had done something so positive. The spirits brought Jim to me, to help me see how this healing worked.

After that I found out that I was there for a few reasons. Another was that Henry wanted to do the first piercing at his own Sundance. He had never been pierced because there had never been anybody qualified to do it. So he asked me if I would. Of course, I couldn't refuse him, I had to do it. We danced the next day and I pierced him.

That morning, Melody and I rested on separate blankets between rounds. When I got up to put my sage crown on, my piercing bones fell out. They were inserted in the side of my crown, so they'd be handy. Melody looked at me, I didn't say anything. She knew that I felt they fell out because I should use them again. She had a sick look on her face.

The next day, I told Henry, I wanted to pierce, last piercing round. During the break, Harold came up to me and said, "Manny, I want to pierce for you, in your place. You've done enough for us already."

Very moved by the gesture, I said, "Harold, you don't have to do that for me, it's my obligation."

"Manny, please, let me have this privilege."

I looked at him for a long, long time, thinking and asking myself if this was something that could be passed to someone else. Harold wouldn't give me a chance to think it over any more. He asked me for my piercing bones.

By this time, Melody was crying and thanked Harold. She was really worried about my health by this time. Melody honored Harold with a special gift, to give thanks. She gave him something that meant a great deal to her. I was deeply moved by my brother Harold's gesture. It created a stronger bond between us. Strangely enough, when Harold was pierced, halfway through the song, the piercings on both sides, suddenly fell off! It was amazing. Neither Harold nor I could believe it, but it made both of us very happy.

We had finished our commitment to Henry's Sundance.

INNER - PURPLE

"Spirit Within"
Spiritually Fulfilled

That Sundance was beautiful. Many people came and honored me. They brought my family many things. I was very humbled by the experience. Here was my second Sundance in one year and well, maybe I'm getting a bit too old for this. Past the half century mark and I'm still dancing like that.

My wife says that it serves as inspiration to the younger people coming up. If they see a guy like me who's diabetic and has high blood pressure, dancing and suffering, it encourages them to go on.

After Henry's Sundance, we made the long journey back home to Ontario, Canada. The trip and our arrival capped the whole summer for us. The remainder of the year was almost a let down. If it hadn't been for friends, it would have been intolerable. I did a few more shows, we made a lot more arts and crafts. We were getting ready for the holiday season.

We had another tragedy strike our family. While coming back from a show in Montreal, I was beginning to have severe pain in my abdomen area. I kept passing it off as indigestion. It grew progressively worse.

Also worth mentioning now, is while driving back from Montreal, I was complaining about my weight. I said to Melody, "Wouldn't it be nice if I could just go in a hospital somewhere and lose weight!" Be careful what you ask for!

This was around the end of October 1992. One evening, after four days of constant pain, I felt I couldn't handle it anymore. The reason we were hesitant to go to the hospital, was because I didn't have any medical insurance. In Canada, every resident has free medical coverage, but I did not have access to it, because of being American.

One evening, I was lying down and didn't want to get up. Melody and the kids were worried. While I was laying there, it came to me to try to heal myself, using the stones I was given. I started praying with them. I asked God, if they really worked, to heal me, not just for myself, but also for my family. Shortly after that, the pain forced me to give in to Melody's wishes and go to the hospital.

When we arrived at Emergency, it wasn't long before they had a look at me. The doctor told me that I was a very sick man, and would not be able to leave. When they told me the cost per day, it almost gave me a heart attack! I started to get up to leave. The doctor told me to hold on, and that something could be worked out financially. He also secretly told me that I could not be refused medical attention and surgery if needed.

I was admitted and remained there for ten days. During that time I contracted pneumonia. Due to that infection, they couldn't remove the gall stones that they had found in my gall bladder. I was on intravenous anti-biotic the entire, stay in the hospital, no food or water. I did lose weight! Twenty-five pounds, in fact.

The infection was so persistent, it kept me from having the gall stones removed. They decided to release me for a couple of weeks until the infection cleared up. The last day before I left, they put me through several more tests. When the doctor in charge of my case came in with the x-rays, he had an astonished look on his face. He couldn't believe what he saw. The gall stones, had dissolved. They simply weren't there any more. They knew I hadn't passed them. He said, in all his years as a doctor, he had never seen anything like it. I tried to explain to him about the healing I had given myself, but he seemed insensitive to what I said. It just went over his head.

Maybe this form of medicine is just too advanced for this technology. Perhaps it is lack of belief. Personally, I knew it was the healing I did on myself that dissolved the gall stones. It didn't really matter whether he believed it or not, I knew my medicine helped me cure myself.

It's like the old expression, "Physician, heal thyself." Meaning the true doctor or man of medicine should be able to heal himself, to offer others methods of healing. I feel the Creator brought me a way to heal myself, to make me realize that I also could help others. It helped me to build confidence in this new way of healing I had received.

I went home to recuperate. The entire ordeal put a tremendous strain on my family and our finances. We mulled over what to do for most of the month.

That winter the Canadian economy started a slow downward slide. Our customers were wary of buying more stock because of the way things were going. Our business was in trouble. Sales were way down, everywhere we went the story was the same. "Your things are beautiful but we're not buying now." I was getting real worried. No sales and the price of food was inching higher and higher every day. It's a sickening feeling to go out day after day and come home with little or no money.

I started praying hard to Grandfather. I asked him to bring me direction, to show me a way to get my family into a better situation. As if by a miracle a very strong line of thought started to invade my mind. At first I didn't want to say anything to anyone. I didn't want to build their hopes up, if I couldn't fulfil what I was thinking. My thoughts kept saying and God kept telling me to move back to the states.

On the afternoon of November 30, when I finally

mentioned it to Melody, a look of delight came over her face.

"If only we could," she cried. "It could be the answer to all my prayers."

The next day was a Friday, we were going to go out again to try to sell. We were facing a pretty slim weekend if we didn't sell anything. We made several calls without success. In desperation I called a store that had called me about a year before. At the time the owner had asked me to bring my crafts by. I don't know why, but I never went to see him. Now I was desperate and searching for an Angel.

We pulled into the mall parking lot in Newmarket, where his store, "Nature's Yard" was and called him from the car phone. Michael came on the line and was really glad to hear from us. He asked us where we were calling from, and we said in the parking lot. He told us to come right up.

He took one look at all the crafts we had, and thought about it a minute. Then he took everything we were holding. He put it to the side and said, "I'll take all this, and triple it for my other two stores as soon as possible." He asked us to balance it out so there was an equal amount for each store.

My head reeling, we started taking inventory of what we had on hand. It was quite a substantial amount. Tripling it answered our prayers for a way to move to the states. Melody was astonished!

An interesting thing started to happen. People came out of the woodwork to buy our crafts. Everything fell into place for us to go. That is usually how you can tell if you're on the right track about something. If you find most things keep going wrong, and there's obstacles everywhere you turn, rethink what you're doing and do something else. You'll know if it's right, if everything goes your way. We knew all this money coming in wasn't to keep us there. It was Grandfather's way to get us going. This all started happening after giving notice on the house.

On December 19, exactly twenty days after deciding to move, we were in the vehicles, on the road to Arizona. In that time we had packed, sold all our furniture, closed our lives in Canada and headed out. It was an emotional time for Melody. She always wanted to move to the States, and now it was happening. She was leaving her friends and family behind to start fresh.

We made it to Arizona on Christmas day. We all arrived at my Mom's house in Ajo. It was a wonderful Christmas, most of my children had never met or knew their grandparents. After losing their Mom, it was good for them to get a sense of family. My sisters and brother all made them feel welcome and loved. It was also the first time Melody met my Mom and Dad. After a couple of days visit, we headed for Phoenix to find our new home.

We have been in a wonderful house since arriving. It's a beautiful four bedroom, with a swimming pool and is everything any of us would want.

It took us about a year to get situated, and get our business off the ground. Unfortunately, when Sundance season came about that summer we didn't have the money to go. Perhaps Grandfather was keeping us from going, for whatever reason. It was very depressing for me. It was the first year I missed the Lakota Sundance since I started. I had to face the fact that I couldn't go.

The rest of the year was spent building up our business and expanding our product line. I found myself on the road more. Phoenix couldn't support us, like Toronto did. This was difficult. Melody had to hold the fort by herself often. We were careful not to be separated for any longer than three weeks. We didn't want the same thing to happen that happened in my previous marriage.

By the spring of 1994, I had made the commitment to go to the Sundance no matter the expense. Even if I had to go by myself, I was going this year. There were so many who wanted to go with me and support our Sundance.

On the first weekend in July, I had an orientation meeting at Marge and Mario's house in Altadena, California for anyone who wanted to attend the Sundance. We found out that weekend there was another Sundance in Colorado, earlier and being put on by the same Sundance Chief, David Swallow. The South Dakota dates were in the middle of August. The one in Colorado was in the middle of July. This made it a better time for us to attend, and financially easier. So we decided to go to Colorado. It was held near the town of Buffalo Creek.

We had two weeks to prepare to go. I had to make a quick sales trip to Northern California. The trip was really hard. Everywhere I went people said they were worried about the economy and didn't have any money. I found it very hard to make a sale, but I was determined to go to the Sundance. Slowly, from a small sale here and another one there, I gathered and saved the money that we needed to go.

We left Phoenix, and the temperature was 115 degrees! We took two vans and pulled our pop-up trailer. My son stayed home, and we went with our five girls. What an adventure! Their energies and temperaments are so different from each other, it made for an interesting and challenging trip - to say the least! I had to handle the reins of that team with one iron fist and one kid glove.

We stopped in Albuquerque to pick up Rose Marie, who wanted to attend the Sundance with us.

She was a healer who I had met, and it was her dream to go. So she came with us and helped with the driving.

We arrived at the Sundance grounds the next evening well before dark. I thought this was amazing. We had left Phoenix the day before around 2:30 in the afternoon. As you can imagine with so many girls, there were many stops along the way. Also we were driving two vans, with one pulling a trailer. We spent the night in Grant's, N.M., leaving early next morning and stopping in Albuquerque. Bear in mind that Albuquerque is over four hundred miles from Denver. It was as though we flew there, because we appeared to get there in record time!

Anyways, the Sundance grounds were absolutely breathtaking! The camping area around the Arbor was all natural. Yet it appeared that Mother Nature had manicured it just for our benefit. The Arbor was big and with fresh cut evergreen boughs laying over the Arbor, offering a wonderful shade. Everyone seemed to hold their breath while looking around. We were all anticipating the next five days. The Rocky Mountains were surrounding us. It was an ideal camping spot.

The Sundance Chief, David Swallow, was very happy to see me with my family. He asked me to set up in a great spot, next to his camp. There was a clear brook running nearby, lots of trees and beautiful landscape. Nature had been busy, making the meeting place for the spirits and the humans a place to remember.

We set up camp and walked around to get acquainted with everyone. There were many people from South Dakota, however, there were a lot from Colorado as well that I didn't know. I reestablished contact with Arnie and Dee Dee, Sundancers from another place, another time, but good friends. It was such a relief for me to be there. All that time I was worried about not being able to make it again. This time, everything fell into place at the last minute.

Sunday was tree day. Rose Marie and Melody had driven into town for supplies and groceries. When it came time to get the tree, excitedly the people in our camp got ready to go. There were a couple of my nephews from California. They had come to pray and offer their support to all the other dancers. There was Big Jon from Los Angeles, Little John from Benecia and Mario who had come to dance and pierce from Pomona and his girlfriend, Taran. Another nephew, Paul from Cerritos came, but he didn't arrive until the following day.

By this time a large crowd was gathering. I called my girls and started following the others. I felt something in my stomach. Some people call it feeling butterflies. To me it was more like a restless spirit within me. A spirit that wanted to be noticed. Not just noticed with indifference, it wanted to be noticed with emotion.

Of all the tree ceremonies I have mentioned so far, this one touched me the most. I don't know if it was because of the loss of my Dad, or if it was the pain that I had felt for my Mother.

This tree seemed to arouse deep feelings in me. I hadn't shed any tears since my Father's passing. But I cried for my Mother's pain and anguish. They had just celebrated their 61st wedding anniversary. Somehow the words that David said at this tree, moved me as no others had. Somehow I related the tree giving its life so we could Sundance, to my Father giving life to four other siblings and me. Suddenly, I felt as if the spirit of my father was within the tree. It was talking to me. As the first axe strike hit the tree, for some inexplicable reason, I felt a deep sorrow for that tree. Perhaps I felt that it was passing on to another life as my dad had done recently.

I know deep inside there was a relationship, I felt the loss of my dad very deeply. For the first time since his passing, tears came to my eyes that were just for him. A part of my sorrow had to do with unresolved differences between my father and I. There would be no other opportunity to talk things over. There had been so many feelings, thoughts and experiences I wanted to talk over with him. Now that wasn't possible.

We had a difficult relationship, the chance to resolve or talk wasn't there. For that reason I was mourning. We should all try to work things out with our parents while they're alive. The day comes when it's too late and you have nothing left but regrets and tears. In my mind and heart, I dedicated this Sundance to my dad's memory.

The tree went up as beautiful and as proud as all the others. Many people, tied their ropes and prayer ties on it. There were many things being asked of the tree. The energy was high around the Arbor.

Finally the tree was up, the ceremony over. We all returned to our camps to prepare for the next day. We left the Sacred Tree alone at last as if to give it the respect and time it needed to prepare itself for us and the next four days.

Monday morning was warm and beautiful. Grandfather had blessed us with a warm and cloudy day. Long before sunrise, Sundancers from all over were gathering around the fire pit, getting ready to go into the Sweat Lodges. Melody and I got up, grabbed our towels and headed down to the same place. I ran into an old Sundance brother and leader, Bo, from South Dakota. Everyone was in a happy and jovial mood. When enough guys were ready to fill the Sweat Lodge, we started the first sweat. It was a good and hot one.

Returning to camp, I started getting ready. When Melody returned she got all her things, including her bedding and moved to the woman's teepee. She was going to be dancing four days, and couldn't return to camp for any reason. I felt a pain in my chest for her because I knew the pain of hunger. I knew the deep knife thrust of thirst that she would be enduring for four, long days.

My heart went out to her, but she wanted to pray and was determined to do it. All I could do, is to be there, be strong for her and help her pray. She was praying for me. That was important to her, and I in turn would pray for her. It's a very hard thing to do, because every Sundancer has nothing personally to gain from being there. Only others to whom the prayers are directed are gaining.

Day one now seems to have gone rather swiftly, but at the time it was long and slow. It's amazing how quickly we forget the pain and the thirst. Several people pierced on the first day. We all danced hard.

There was one lady, Anna Mae, who pierced both her wrists that first day. She had made a commitment to stay pierced for the entire four days. She was doing it for her husband, Leonard Peltier, who unfortunately was in prison. He's there for something that's been proven that he didn't do. Many people's heart and mine went out to her and for him. Not many women would stand by their husband or mate like that. It's a big sacrifice and extremely hard. He is a fortunate man.

The second was harder. Everyone was thirstier and hungry. I had a commitment to drag buffalo skulls. I had thought to do it on the last day. The more I thought about it, I decided that I should do it then, on the second day, while I still had the strength.

That morning after getting up, I saw my baby girl, Oriona. As I picked her up to hold her, she nuzzled me with her nose and gave me a kiss on the cheek and asked, "Daddy, can I dance with you today?"

I'm not sure if she remembered the time I carried her in the Sundance. It was almost as if she knew that I was going to be dragging skulls.

It really touched me. As I embraced her I said to her, "Sure you can honey, you're gonna dance with Daddy."

So after going in, we put our pipes on the altar and the dancing started in earnest. The very first piercing round was the round for me to drag the skulls. Right away I got my back marked to show where I wanted to be pierced. I told David and Bo that I wanted to stay pierced and wanted to drag the skulls. I wanted to be pierced deep. I wanted to try to drag the skulls all four rounds. There were eight of them and they were fairly large.

They took me to the tree to pray, after a couple of minutes, a Sundance leader asked me if I was ready. I nodded, yes. I walked over and stood on the buffalo hide. With David on one side and Bo on the other, I handed them my piercing bones. I felt David grab the flesh on my back. I felt the knife cut into my back, but my prayers were so deep and intense there was very little pain. By the time it was Bo's turn to pierce my right side, my prayers for strength were being answered - I didn't feel a thing.

Suddenly as if awakening, I felt both of them grab my arms and lead me toward the west side of the arbor. Melody handed me my baby, Oriona. She was smiling and looking around at everyone, with a curiosity on her face rather than fright.

There were sixteen warriors, carrying the eight skulls behind me. David believes that each man dragging skulls should at least make one complete circle with the skulls attached to his back. Therefore he had the skulls carried by the warriors, one full circle around the arbor. While we were dancing, I heard someone say, "*Wamblee*, Eagle!" I raised my head and saw directly above us, two beautiful Spotted Eagles circling the Arbor. Since I was dancing, I couldn't keep looking at them, but I was told that they disappeared into the sun. I was really honored to have their presence while I danced and pierced. This is considered very powerful medicine. It means that all my prayers will be answered and anyone praying with me will have their prayers answered.

Getting back around to the west side, they put down the skulls and it was my time to move them by myself. As I started leaning into the rope, at first I felt like I was trying to pull the world. Ever so slightly I felt the skulls start to move. Then suddenly the left side broke loose. My thoughts were, I didn't want to break yet, I wanted to drag the skulls. So as carefully as I could I continued pulling with my other side. The weight was too much, my right side broke loose as the skulls started to move again. I suppose Grandfather didn't want me to go through the pain and suffering required to move that kind of weight.

When I broke loose, I yelled with joy and ran around the Arbor, holding the baby. This was my third time dragging skulls and I was happy to have made it through again.

I returned my baby girl, Oriona to my wife, then to the center of the Arbor, the Sacred Tree. After praying and giving thanks at the tree, David and Bo were waiting for me to get through with my prayers. When I was through they turned me around. The pieces of flesh that were hanging off my back, were cut off and placed in small pieces of red cloth. They were my flesh offerings and were tied to the tree.

Many people ask me, why do you pierce? What is the significance of your piercing? Why do you mutilate your body like this?

It's not a mutilation or self-torture. It is our way, our very sacred way of giving a small piece of the only thing we truly own, our bodies. We feel that anything other than the body, is something material that we can live without.

Flesh, blood and pain is all we truly own. This is the flesh of the body that houses our spirit and soul. It's a way to give our living flesh to the spirit world, so they will listen to our prayers and pleas.

More guys pierced and prayed and broke loose. It was a beautiful Sundance, the singers' voices were still strong. We had two drums singing all the sacred songs for us. Again we were blessed with a partly cloudy sky. When the sun was out and hot, Grandfather would always bring us a cloud to cool us off a bit.

Now is a good time to mention how this Sundance affected my health. I had been on blood pressure pills for several years and diabetes pills since 1991. My wife was very concerned about this, because we had accidentally forgotten the high blood pressure pills. At high altitudes my blood pressure would get very high. My head would start buzzing, and I'd get very sick.

When we were dancing, Melody and several others were praying I could overcome this illness. Another thing was the diabetes, I was on three pills a day. All the prayers for me have been answered. Since the Sundance, I haven't taken any blood pressure pills and am down to one diabetes pill.

The third day was the healing ceremony. On this third day, one of my twin daughters, Becky also joined us in the Sundance arbor. She had wanted to dance all four days. As an old experienced

Sundancer, I knew how hard this was, so I convinced her only to dance the last two days.

It seemed like all the people who were there to support us, gathered around the Arbor for healing from the Sundancers. We believe that within the sacred circle, every Sundancer who willingly went in to suffer and give of himself, has the right to be a healing tool. That Sundancer earned the right, during that special day, to offer healing with the Creator's blessing. Every dancer slowly proceeded around the Arbor, doing their best to help the people who were lined up. The ceremony was beautiful and many people cried when the Sundancers prayed for them. It was an emotional time.

It lasted about four hours. When we were getting our pipes from the altar, while we were dancing Melody looked up and saw a cloud. It was formed in the exact shape of a buffalo skull. When she pointed it out, several other dancers also looked and saw it. It was clear, there was no doubting that it was a buffalo skull. It was a good medicine sign, which meant strength and abundance for everyone. The day was longer than usual, we didn't get out of the Arbor until late, long after dark.

Day three was over and everyone was tired and I could tell the thirst was taking its toll on everyone. I could see Melody suffering quite a bit. Incidentally, it was Melody's birthday as well and she was happy to be helping others and to be where she was on her special day. Becky was having a very hard time; she hadn't realized how hard David's Sundance is. By the end of the first day she was happy that she had only committed to two days.

The final day arrived, and it was the hottest day since the Sundance had started. The morning was beautiful, bright and sunny. We were told the day would be shorter than the others. Everyone was happy, they had all undergone a very challenging trial and had made it. Many others joined on the last day to dance. They were people who had only made a one day commitment.

The helpers and Sundance leaders had to pierce on the last piercing round, which included me. When the time came for us to pierce, we all gathered in the center. First one, then the other until all the Sundance leaders had been pierced. I wanted Melody to be with me when I pierced, so I asked the women's Sundance leader, Pansy, to bring Melody to the tree. She brought Melody a couple of minutes before. She thought that I would be laying down to pierce; she told Melody to get on her knees. As I said before, today was the hottest day. When Melody knelt down, her knees landed on the small pebbles that were so hot, her knees blistered and burned.

When they pierced me, we all moved to the southwest side of the Arbor. I was happy to see Rose Marie, all my daughters, Stormy, Mary, Dory and Oriona. My nephews, John, Jon and Paul - they were all there supporting me. We danced until it was time to break loose. There were four of us piercing this last round. We all broke loose. Al and Bernice's son, Richard, was called in to do the piercing on David. He danced strong and hard, while dragging the skulls. It's very hard to drag skulls very far when they are so heavy and there are so many.

During the last couple of rounds, your mind races frantically. Who still needed prayers, or who may I have missed? You realize that the time to Sundance is ending until next year. Although you can pray to the Creator anytime, it's as though your prayers are stronger during this sacred ceremony. I'm sure everyone goes through this experience, suddenly the four days are over.

Since this was David's last time to Sundance in

this Arbor in Colorado, it was a very special year for him. You could see he was leaving a part of himself behind, as others had before him. They had lost their Sundance Chief to the Creator, and asked David to run the Sundance for them. This was his fourth and last year. His commitment to the Denver people was complete. They must now choose another Sundance Chief.

It's over, thank God. I have now survived fourteen Sundances in ten years and been pierced many times. I was grateful for the opportunity and proud to Sundance with the Shoshoni, Lakota and members of all the other tribes I have danced with.

The Sundance was God sent to me. The Creator gave me something that would please me and fulfil my spiritual cravings. I thank the Creator every day for bringing me the Sundance and the Ceremonial Pipe. I found what had always been there for me, all I had to do, was look and ask. I searched all over and in other beliefs yet I had overlooked at what was natively mine. It's so simple now.

I had finally found a spiritual awareness within myself. I was content with what I had found! I also felt a great weight lifted from my spirit. Although the Spirit itself has no substance or physical restraints, I believe that when our Spirits are without direction or focus, there is a great, almost physical stress put on our lives. Until we find our individual spirituality.

That spiritual stress then invades our physical body, creating an uneasy restlessness. We find ourselves always looking for that spiritual relief. We find ourselves searching until we get something we're content with. Some people choose Buddhism, Christianity and some feel comfortable with Hinduism. There is something for everyone. It's just a matter of feeling good about what you find.

I've committed myself to the Chanupa, the

Sacred Pipe. I have committed myself to Sundancing every year, as long as I live. Unfortunately, I wish I could follow this year around, but it's very hard because of our life style. Many of us tend to forget our spirituality until we are in need of help.

However, the Sundance is never forgotten in my home. Every meal we give thanks. Sometimes we hold hands and form a prayer circle. Sometimes we don't. Every meal I give thanks to the Creator for having given it to me. Every time I wake up, I give thanks that I am here for my children one more day. I don't ever know what that day is going to bring, but I hope that it will always bring tranquillity to the world and peace to my family.

I always pray that people stop and realize what we are doing to our Mother Earth. I realize that people are busy and are going about their lives. They don't seem to care about anything, except what is important to them. We should stop to realize that this is the only world we've got. This planet we are standing on, is like our heart. This planet that we abuse daily. It's our heart. Without it we don't have a life! We don't survive. We don't exist.

Again and for the last time I want to ask you that same question I have asked. Why did God or the Creator decide to create us humans?

Here is my answer to that question.

I believe that a God, the Creator needs us to worship him. Without us, he doesn't exist. No God is a God if he has no one to acknowledge him. I believe that since he needs us to recognize him as a god, it's his obligation to take care of us. In this way, he pays us back for our worship, by answering our prayers. We can demand his help, and he has an obligation to give it to us. Our obligation is to worship and show respect.

I wonder sometimes, why it took me so long to

find the Sundance. It seemed there were so many times in my life, when I would have been a better person had I been Sundancing.

As one Sundance Chief told me, it's very possible that I was just not ready and the Spirits wanted me to wait until I was.

Now that you have finished reading this, you have knowledge that places you on a higher spiritual plateau. Make a commitment to yourself, always walk in balance and not judge others. Be grateful for the things you receive and always remember to give in return.

This journey has been a long and hard one for me, but in a good way. You have witnessed my hopes, fears, desires, feelings and the baring of my soul. All this was necessary as it led me to . . .

My road to the Sundance.

Should you wish any further information on the Sundance or would like to contribute to a non-profit organization, the Native American Spirituality Association would be glad to answer any of your questions. All donations are tax deductible and very much needed.

Native American Spirituality
Association of Colorado
c/o David Waltrip
1133 Cranbrook Court
Boulder, Colorado
80303

If you cannot find a copy of this book in your local bookstore or library, you can order by calling 1-800-786-6322 , or by mail:

Wo-Pila Publishing
P.O. Box 84002
Phoenix, Arizona
85071-4002